THE SAN FRANCISCO EARTHQUAKE AND FIRE
OF 1906

GREAT HISTORIC DISASTERS

The Atomic Bombings of Hiroshima
and Nagasaki

The Black Death

The Dust Bowl

The Great Chicago Fire of 1871

The *Hindenburg* Disaster of 1937

Hurricane Katrina

The Indian Ocean Tsunami of 2004

The Influenza Pandemic of 1918–1919

The Johnstown Flood of 1889

The San Francisco Earthquake and Fire
of 1906

The Sinking of the *Titanic*

The Triangle Shirtwaist Factory Fire

GREAT HISTORIC DISASTERS

THE SAN FRANCISCO EARTHQUAKE AND FIRE OF 1906

LOUISE CHIPLEY SLAVICEK

CHELSEA HOUSE
PUBLISHERS

An imprint of Infobase Publishing

THE SAN FRANCISCO EARTHQUAKE AND FIRE OF 1906

Chelsea House
An imprint of Infobase Publishing
132 West 31st Street
New York, NY 10001

Library of Congress Cataloging-in-Publication Data
Slavicek, Louise Chipley, 1956-
The San Francisco earthquake and fire of 1906 / Louise Chipley Slavicek.
   p.   cm.—(Great historic disasters)
Includes bibliographical references and index.
ISBN: 978-0-7910-9650-5 (hardcover)
1. San Francisco Earthquake and Fire, Calif., 1906—Juvenile literature.
2. Earthquakes—California—San Francisco—History—20th century—
Juvenile literature. 3. Fires—California—San Francisco—History—20th
century—Juvenile literature. 4. San Francisco (Calif.)—History—20th
century—Juvenile literature. I. Title. II. Series.
F869.S357S537 2008
979.4'61051—dc22   2008004896

Chelsea House books are available at special discounts when purchased in bulk quantities for businesses, associations, institutions, or sales promotions. Please call our Special Sales Department in New York at (212) 967-8800 or (800) 322-8755.

You can find Chelsea House on the World Wide Web
at http://www.chelseahouse.com

Text design by Annie O'Donnell
Cover design by Ben Peterson

Printed in the United States of America

Bang KT 10 9 8 7 6 5 4 3 2 1

This book is printed on acid-free paper.

All links and Web addresses were checked and verified to be correct at the time of publication. Because of the dynamic nature of the Web, some addresses and links may have changed since publication and may no longer be valid.

Contents

Introduction: A City in Ruins   7

1 San Francisco on the Eve of Disaster   13

2 Wednesday, April 18, 1906, 5:12 A.M.   27

3 Earthquake Science in 1906 and Today   40

4 San Francisco in Flames   54

5 The Battle for San Francisco Continues   66

6 Coping with the Catastrophe   77

7 Rebuilding   90

8 Into the Future   102

Chronology and Timeline   112

Glossary   115

Bibliography   118

Further Reading   121

Picture Credits   122

Index   123

About the Author   128

Introduction:
A City in Ruins

At approximately 5:12 A.M. on Wednesday, April 18, 1906, the city of San Francisco began to shudder. Roadways rose and fell like ocean waves. Crumbling walls and chimneys rained glass and bricks onto sidewalks and streets. In those parts of the city built on loose, mushy landfill, the shaken soil turned to liquid, and crowded rooming houses suddenly vanished into heaps of splintered wood, trapping their terrified inhabitants within.

At 5:12, police sergeant Jesse Cook was walking his beat in San Francisco's already bustling produce district. Later, he recalled the chaos and horror of that spring morning, when the deadliest earthquake in U.S. history roared into his hometown: "The noise and the dust, and the feeling of destruction, all combined to daze a man," Cook remembered. "All about us houses were tumbling, and falling walls and chimneys, and cornices were crushing men and horses in the street. The district at that hour was crowded with produce wagons, and through the uproar of the earthquake, you could hear the cries of people and the whinnying of the horses that were hurt. . . ." Although Sergeant Cook could not have imagined it then, San Francisco's terrible ordeal had only begun.

The violent trembling of the ground, the result of a nearly 300-mile-long rupture on California's famous San Andreas Fault, had hardly stilled when fires started to ignite throughout the stricken city. As the morning wore on, crossed electrical wires, overturned lamps and wood stoves, damaged chimneys, and severed gas lines sparked dozens of blazes. Firefighters

Due to a series of fortuitous events, the budding California town of San Francisco quickly became a booming port city. In 1906, an earthquake and subsequent fire forever changed the city.

raced for the nearest hydrants only to discover they were dry: The quake had shattered the underground supply pipes that carried water into the city from distant reservoirs.

Fed by earthquake debris and fanned by strong winds, the blazes quickly became an unstoppable inferno, incinerating everything in their path. Desperate to slow the conflagration's advance, city officials authorized army demolition teams to blow up entire blocks of buildings in hopes of creating fire-breaks, a tragically misguided strategy that only served to spread the flames further. For three days and nights, the fires raged, devouring virtually the entire downtown district and many of San Francisco's most populous residential neighbor-hoods. By the time the blazes were finally brought under control early on Saturday, April 21, 500 city blocks lay in ruins and 225,000 San Franciscans were homeless. The inferno sparked by the quake of April 18 remains the worst urban fire in U.S. history, larger and more destructive even than the notorious Chicago fire of 1871.

In the wake of the devastating earthquake and fire, the once vibrant city of San Francisco was a blackened waste-land of gutted and crumpled buildings and ash. It looked, observed writer Jack London, "like the crater of a volcano." The temblor and resultant fire of April 1906 was the first major disaster to receive extensive photographic coverage, and millions of people all over the world marveled at images of the greatest American metropolis west of the Mississippi reduced to smoldering rubble. Only a few years earlier, the Eastman Kodak Company had introduced the Brownie, the first mass-produced, inexpensive camera, and in the calamity's wake, scores of professional and amateur photographers alike poured onto San Francisco's streets to document the shocking destruction.

Until Hurricane Katrina slammed into the Gulf Coast in 2005, the San Francisco earthquake and ensuing con-flagration of April 1906 was the biggest natural disaster to hit U.S. soil. Modern estimates place the cataclysm's death toll at 3,000, with tens of thousands more seriously injured. Property damage in the San Francisco Bay Area totaled at least $400 million—more than $8 billion in current U.S. dollars. Yet, amazingly, despite the almost unfathomable scope of the disaster, within just three years San Franciscans had

Facts and Figures:
The San Francisco Earthquake and Fire of April 18–April 21, 1906

60–65 seconds
estimated length of the earthquake that struck San Francisco at 5:12 A.M.

72 hours
how long the fires lasted following the earthquake

3,000
estimated fatalities from the earthquake and fire

28,800
of San Francisco's 53,000 buildings were destroyed in the disaster

225,000
of San Francisco's approximately 400,000 inhabitants were left homeless

$400 million
in property damage (about $8.2 billion in today's dollars) throughout the city

managed to almost completely rebuild their city, erecting 20,000 new homes, libraries, schools, factories, offices, and other structures to replace the 28,800 buildings leveled by the earthquake and fire. Thus, the story of the great San Francisco calamity of 1906 is not only a chronicle of horror, suffering, and loss but also one of unflagging resilience, courage, and hope.

1

San Francisco on the Eve of Disaster

On the eve of the catastrophic earthquake and fire of April 1906, the city of San Francisco was thriving. With a population of more than 400,000, the so-called City by the Bay was the ninth-largest metropolis in the United States and the largest west of St. Louis. Situated on the tip of the hilly peninsula that separates San Francisco Bay from the Pacific Ocean, in 1906 San Francisco was not only the busiest port on the Pacific coast but also the financial, commercial, and cultural hub of the entire American West.

THE RISE OF SAN FRANCISCO

Spain's exploration and colonization of the Americas began with the arrival of Christopher Columbus in the Caribbean in 1492. It was not until 1769, however, that the Spaniards caught their first glimpse of San Francisco Bay during a naval expedition along California's Pacific Coast. When the expedition's leader, Captain Don Gaspar de Portolá, spotted the craggy tip of San Francisco Peninsula, he sent a small scouting party to investigate. The men were unimpressed by what they found. The promontory was short on freshwater and wood, they declared, and would make a poor place to plant a colony. In light of this discouraging report, Portolá decided to explore the area no further. Nearly a decade after Portolá's expedition, in 1776, the Spanish government finally recognized the potential value of the peninsula and 500-square-mile bay as a military base and port. That year, the crown established a fort, the Presidio, on the northwestern end of the peninsula and a Catholic mission several miles to the south of the stronghold.

Yet Spain was not destined to hold onto its new harbor and military base for long. When Mexico won its independence from Spain in 1821, San Francisco Peninsula—along with the rest of California—was absorbed into the Mexican Empire. Soon after, a tiny settlement named Yerba Buena ("Good Herb") sprang up in the wind-swept hills between the Presidio and the old Spanish mission to its south. Just 25 years later, the peninsula—and the sleepy village of Yerba Buena—changed hands again when the U.S. government laid claim to all of California during the Mexican-American War (1846–1848). In 1850, Yerba Buena—under its new name of San Francisco—officially became part of the United States when California was admitted as the nation's 31st state.

Two years earlier, in 1848, the history of San Francisco had been forever changed when gold was found at Sutter's Mill in California's Sierra Nevada. As news of the lucrative discovery spread during the following year, gold hunters—or "forty-niners" as the prospectors were nicknamed—descended on California from all parts of the United States as well as Europe, Asia, Australia, and Latin America. The great California Gold Rush was on, and its impact on San Francisco was dramatic. The port of San Francisco became the gateway into the interior for many of the tens of thousands of fortune seekers who made their way to California by sea, and virtually overnight, the remote hamlet of 800 inhabitants was transformed into a bustling city. By 1850, San Francisco's population had ballooned to more than 25,000, and dozens of boardinghouses, hotels, restaurants, stores, banks, and saloons had sprouted up all over the city to serve the hard-spending newcomers' every need.

THE FINANCIAL, COMMERCIAL, AND CULTURAL CAPITAL OF THE WEST

When the Gold Rush finally ended in 1855, most forty-niners had not even found enough of the precious metal to cover their expenses. Thousands of the former prospectors decided to stay in San Francisco: some because they lacked the money to buy

In 1848, the discovery of gold provided a reason for people to settle in California. Men from all over the world arrived by the boatload in San Francisco and headed to the mountains to find their fortune. Mining camps became mining towns, filling up with men looking for even the tiniest nuggets of gold.

passage home, others because they had simply taken a liking to the dynamic young city.

In 1859, a huge deposit of silver—the Comstock Lode—was discovered to the east of California in the Nevada territory. The new "silver rush" was destined to have almost as dramatic an impact on San Francisco as the earlier Gold Rush had had. Once again, swarms of treasure seekers disembarked at the port of San Francisco, and much of the estimated $400 million yielded by the Comstock Lode ended up

Mark Twain and the San Francisco Earthquake of 1865

On October 8, 1865, while he was working as a newspaper reporter in San Francisco, Mark Twain experienced his first temblor. Although considerably weaker than the 1906 earthquake, the earthquake of 1865 brought down chimneys and cracked walls. Twain's description of the earthquake is excerpted from his book *Roughing It,* first published in 1872.

It was just after noon, on a bright October day. I was coming down Third Street. The only objects in motion anywhere . . . were a man in a buggy behind me, and a [horse-drawn] streetcar wending slowly up the cross street. . . .

As I turned the corner, around a frame house, there was a great rattle and jar. . . . Before I could turn and seek the door, there came a terrific shock; the ground seemed to roll under me in waves, interrupted by a violent joggling up and down, and there was a heavy grinding noise as of in San Francisco banks or invested in the city's burgeoning manufacturing, shipping, and retail enterprises. San Francisco's importance as a commercial hub was further enhanced when the Bay Area became the terminus (end point) of the first transcontinental railroad in 1869.

By the beginning of the twentieth century, San Francisco had emerged as the undisputed economic capital of the American West. Magnificent restaurants, theaters, shops, hotels, and office buildings to serve the city's growing number

brick houses rubbing together. I fell up against the frame house and hurt my elbow. . . A third and still severer shock came, and as I reeled about on the pavement trying to keep my footing, I saw a sight! The entire front of a tall four-story brick building on Third Street sprung outward like a door and fell sprawling across the street, raising a great dust-like volume of smoke!

And here came the buggy—overboard went the man, and in less time than I can tell it the vehicle was distributed in small fragments along three hundred yards of street. . . . The streetcar had stopped, the horses were rearing and plunging, the passengers were pouring out at both ends. . . . Every door, of every house, as far as the eye could reach, was vomiting a stream of human beings; and almost before one could execute a wink and begin another, there was a massed multitude of people stretching in endless procession down every street my position commanded. . . .

For some days afterward, groups of eyeing and pointing men stood about many a building, looking at long zig-zag cracks that extended from the eaves to the ground. . . .

of well-to-do bankers, entrepreneurs, speculators, and lawyers lined the streets of San Francisco's bustling downtown area. North and west of the downtown on Nob Hill and Van Ness Avenue, the wealthy built sumptuous mansions in the graceful and highly ornate Victorian style of architecture. San Francisco's upper crust also campaigned successfully for the creation of Golden Gate Park to the west of the city, a spacious and beautiful public place designed to rival New York City's famed Central Park.

Prosperous San Franciscans also hoped to make their city the equal of New York in the realm of culture. By 1880, the city possessed one of the biggest opera houses in the nation and more than a dozen theaters. Sarah Bernhardt, Edwin Booth, and other leading actors of the era made the long railroad journey west to perform on San Francisco's stages, and on April 17, 1906, only hours before the earthquake struck, world-renowned tenor, Enrico Caruso, sang before an audience of 3,000 at the Grand Opera House on Mission Street. Literature as well as music and drama flourished in the Bay City, which was home to Mark Twain, Jack London, Bret Harte, and Robert Louis Stevenson, among other notable American writers, at one time or another during the late nineteenth and early twentieth centuries.

SOUTH OF THE SLOT, CHINATOWN, AND THE BARBARY COAST

While San Francisco's wealthy elite resided in palatial mansions and wiled away their leisure time attending the opera or theater or dining at one of the city's many fine restaurants, the members of San Francisco's large and ethnically diverse laboring class were leading a very different kind of existence. Many workers, particularly recent Irish and German immigrants, toiled and lived south of the downtown in an area popularly called "South of the Slot," where drab warehouses, factories, and railroad yards were interspersed with cramped wood-frame houses and rickety boardinghouses. Most of the city's large Italian population lived in equally humble dwellings on the opposite side of the downtown in the North Beach District, otherwise known as the Latin Quarter.

Also located to the north of San Francisco's downtown was the biggest Chinese community outside of Asia in the year 1906: Chinatown. Because of the infamous Chinese Exclusion Act of 1882, most of the neighborhood's estimated 25,000 inhabitants were aging single males who had first come to California decades earlier to work on the railroads and escape the grinding

The Barbary Coast area of San Francisco gained a reputation for lawlessness and immorality. Located on the waterfront, the neighborhood's saloons and dancehalls gave sailors and shady characters venues to engage in wild behavior, much to the shock and indignation of upright citizens living in nearby neighborhoods.

poverty of their homeland. The Chinese Exclusion Act had its roots in the economic anxieties of white Westerners, who pressured Congress to approve the law because they feared an influx of impoverished Chinese willing to work for low pay would cause wages to decline for all Americans.

Even after the passage of the Exclusion Act, white prejudice against the Chinese remained high in San Francisco and elsewhere in the West. Consequently, while many of San Francisco's Chinese inhabitants worked outside of Chinatown, usually as servants to well-to-do whites, racist local laws prevented them from buying a home or even renting a room beyond the crowded, rat-infested confines of the 12-square-block district.

Over the years, Chinatown had developed a certain degree of notoriety for its many underground opium dens and gambling houses. (Opium is a highly habit-forming drug made from a certain type of poppy.) Nonetheless, ever since the days of the Gold Rush, San Francisco's most disreputable district had been the Barbary Coast, named after the infamous, pirate-infested coast of North Africa. Located along the city's busy waterfront, the Barbary Coast was the favorite district of the throngs of sailors on leave who passed through San Francisco's port. It was known for its raucous saloons, tawdry dancehalls, cheap rooming houses, and large criminal element. A world away from the genteel neighborhoods of Van Buren Avenue or Nob Hill, the rough-and-tumble district appalled respectable middle- and upper-class San Franciscans, who considered Barbary Coast as a blot on the city's good name.

"OILING THE SKIDS": POLITICS IN SAN FRANCISCO

San Francisco on the eve of the great earthquake, like many other big cities in the United States during the early twentieth century, suffered from rampant political corruption. For decades, city officials had been offering favors, including political appointments and government contracts, in return for lucrative kickbacks. Yet, under the direction of San Francisco's mayor since 1901, Eugene Schmitz and his political mentor and personal attorney, Abraham (Abe) Ruef, graft—the use of political power for personal gain—had become more widespread and blatant among the city's leadership.

Despite his administration's sordid reputation, Schmitz was remarkably successful in winning and maintaining the loyalty of San Francisco's voting public. Indeed, during the November 1905 elections, the mayor's Labor Union Party won every single seat on the Board of Supervisors, the 11-member legislative branch of the City and County of San Francisco. Even Schmitz's cohort Ruef had to admit that the newly elected board members were so hungry for "boodle" (bribes) that "they would eat the paint off a house."

Schmitz's continuing popularity with his constituents does not surprise historian William Bronson. After all, pointed out Bronson, in his book *The Earth Shook, The Sky Burned*, in San Francisco "'oiling the skids'"—in other words, bribery and extortion—"had been part of doing business with City Hall for a long time." Moreover, by all accounts, Schmitz, a well-known concert violinist and orchestra conductor, was remarkably charismatic. Tall and broad-shouldered with thick black hair and piercing blue eyes, "Handsome Gene," as the mayor was nicknamed, was invariably charming, self-assured, and unflappable in all his dealings with the public. Abe Ruef, who first persuaded Schmitz, a high-school dropout, to run for San Francisco's top office, characterized the mayor as a man of "natural ability [and] . . . keen perception. He possessed a tenacious memory and insuperable [unconquerable] nerve. He could assume a pretense which successfully covered up all deficiencies. His face completely masked his real feelings."

After five years at the helm of the city government, Schmitz and his right-hand man, Ruef, commanded enormous

San Francisco's Famous Cable Cars

The area south of San Francisco's downtown, the so-called South of the Slot district, got its name from what has become one of the city's best-known and beloved symbols: the cable car. Cable cars are passenger vehicles that operate on rails. A continuously moving underground cable that runs in a "slot," or groove, between the rail tracks propels the cars. The phrase "South of the Slot" referred to the slot in the middle of the cable car tracks that ran along the major downtown thoroughfare of Market Street.

Cable cars were the brainchild of Andrew Hallidie, a British immigrant to California and a mining engineer. Supposedly, Hallidie was inspired to create the new mode of mass transit after witnessing a San Francisco horse-car driver savagely whip his team of horses as they struggled to pull their heavy load up a steep incline. (A horse car was a long passenger vehicle pulled by horses.) The first cable-

personal wealth and power. Any local company, organization, or individual requesting government assistance was first routed to Ruef's law office, wrote Kurzman in *Disaster!*, and "no contract was authorized without a kickback, no franchise approved without a personal fee . . . . The two city kingpins also pocketed a cut from the earnings of the telephone and telegraph companies and the city's public transportation system. And they tapped into public works, liquor licenses, . . . restaurant franchises, gambling, public buildings, road-paving contracts, [and] construction permits." Rumor had it that the mayor kept his ill-gotten money in a plush-lined "boodle box" car line opened in San Francisco in 1873, and by the end of the century, the hilly city had more than 20 lines, covering dozens of miles. Cable cars were also installed in other big cities around the world, including Chicago, New York, Sydney, and Paris.

The heyday of the cable car, however, would prove fleeting. By the early twentieth century, most cities had switched over to electric streetcars, or trolleys, which were not only faster but also cheaper to build and operate. In San Francisco, streetcars largely replaced cable cars after the 1906 earthquake, which destroyed much of the city's cable tracks. Nonetheless, San Franciscans were reluctant to give up entirely the transportation system that had gotten its start in their home city. Consequently, more than a century after the quake, the city still boasts three cable-car lines. The brightly colored vehicles have become one of San Francisco's major tourist attractions and are the only operating cables cars remaining in the world today.

that had been especially built into the bedroom floor of his ornate, Victorian-style mansion.

FIRE CHIEF SULLIVAN VERSUS CITY HALL

Schmitz and Ruef's stranglehold over the city seemed all but unassailable. They not only controlled the Board of Supervisors but also several prominent judges and the chief of police. One man they could not control, however, was San Francisco's outspoken fire chief, Dennis Sullivan. Sullivan had been fighting with City Hall over increased funding for the city's firefighting facilities and particularly for its water system, which the fire chief feared would prove woefully inadequate in a large fire. Sullivan had cause for concern. During the mid-nineteenth century, the windy City by the Bay had burned down no less than six times. After the last big conflagration, many of the wood buildings in the city's commercial district had been replaced with brick and stone structures. However, as of 1906, fully 90 percent of the city's structures were still wooden framed and therefore highly flammable.

Convinced that another major fire was inevitable, Sullivan wanted to supplement the city's existing hydrant system, which drew on freshwater reservoirs several miles outside of San Francisco, with a saltwater system capable of pumping

San Francisco firefighters struggle to contain the blaze that erupted after the great earthquake. The cheap and easy-to-build wooden structures that dotted the city only fueled the fire.

large amounts of water from the nearby bay. He also wanted to repair and refill the city's 63 long-neglected cisterns—large underground tanks for storing water. The huge metal tubs had been buried beneath San Francisco's heavily built downtown area decades earlier to provide an auxiliary water supply for the fire department, and then promptly forgotten by the Board of Public Works, the governmental agency supposedly responsible for maintaining them.

Yet, to Chief Sullivan's immense frustration, while there always seemed to be plenty of money floating around City Hall for other projects, somehow the mayor and the Board of Supervisors could never find the funds to upgrade the city's critically important firefighting system. According to author Dennis Smith, City Hall's unwillingness to come to the aid of the fire department probably had much to do with Sullivan's well-known disdain for "oiling the skids." Noted Smith in *San Francisco Is Burning: The Untold Story of the 1906 Earthquake and Fires*, among all the directors of the various city agencies in San Francisco, only Dennis Sullivan

> made it a policy to list in the annual municipal reports every significant dollar allocation made to persons, firms, and corporations doing business with . . . [his] department. Dennis Sullivan was keenly aware that the city's political powers would skin the hide off a nickel's buffalo if they could, and this annual transparency in the city's report made the fire department's reputation for honesty secure and prevented, by the power of public scrutiny, the possibility of inflated charges for goods and services.

A CRUSADE TO TOPPLE SCHMITZ AND RUEF

Fire chief Sullivan was not alone in his frustration with City Hall on the eve of the great earthquake. Fremont Older, the editor of the *San Francisco Bulletin*, had been attacking the

Schmitz administration's dishonest practices in his newspaper for years. When the people of San Francisco nonetheless reelected Schmitz to a third term in November 1905, Older was incensed.

Grimly determined to topple "Handsome Gene" and his chief partner in crime, Abe Ruef, Older made the long train journey to Washington, D.C. The newspaperman was on a mission: He intended to persuade the nation's reformist president, Theodore Roosevelt, to launch a major federal probe into Schmitz and Ruef's shady financial dealings. Much impressed by Older's intelligence and zeal, Roosevelt agreed to lend him the services of two highly experienced federal employees, one a Secret Service agent and the other a special prosecutor. Roosevelt, however, told Older that he would have to scrape together the money to pay for the investigation. By February 1906, Older had persuaded his close friend Rudolph Spreckels, one of San Francisco's wealthiest citizens and a passionate supporter of clean government, to bankroll his crusade to bring down Schmitz and Ruef.

On April 17, 1906, two months after Spreckels joined Older's campaign, Eugene Schmitz learned for the first time that he was being investigated for corruption. One of the mayor's own appointees, San Francisco District Attorney William Langdon, had already begun to assemble evidence of graft and bribery against Schmitz and his crony Ruef. It certainly looked as though "Handsome Gene's" luck was about to run out. Then at approximately 5:12 on the morning of Wednesday, April 18, the unimaginable happened.

2 Wednesday, April 18, 1906, 5:12 A.M.

Between approximately **5:12 and 5:13 on the** morning of April 18, 1906, a massive earthquake ripped through the city of San Francisco. The San Francisco earthquake of 1906 was not the most powerful earthquake to strike the United States. Yet because it occurred nearer to a major population center than any other North American earthquake, in terms of lives and property lost the temblor remains the worst natural disaster of its kind in U.S. history.

FIRST ENCOUNTERS WITH THE EARTHQUAKE

The first people to encounter the deadly earthquake that ravaged San Francisco on April 18, 1906, were not on land. Rather they were the startled crewmembers of American and foreign merchant ships plying the waters near northern California's Pacific coastline. Also alerted was one very frightened San Franciscan who was taking an early morning dip in the breakers off Ocean Beach, just to the south of Golden Gate Park. The sailors and the swimmer were the first to feel the temblor's effects on that fateful Wednesday morning because they happened to be closest to its epicenter—the point on the Earth's surface directly above where an earthquake originates. Today, scientists agree that the destructive temblor originated beneath the floor of the Pacific Ocean near San Francisco Peninsula's western coastline. Although the precise location of the quake's underwater epicenter remains a matter of debate among scholars, in recent years many researchers have placed it one or two miles west of Golden Gate Park.

When he first felt the fierce shaking shortly after 5:00 A.M. on April 18, 1906, like many sailors in the waters off San Francisco Peninsula that morning, the chief engineer of the *National City* assumed his steamship had struck a huge rock or submerged wreck. "The ship seemed to jump clear out of the water, the engines raced fearfully, as though the shaft or wheel had gone, and then a violent trembling fore and aft and sideways, reminding me of running full speed against a wall of ice," the perplexed engineer noted in his log (ship's record). A short distance away, another steamship, the *Wellington*, was approaching the entrance to San Francisco Bay at 5:12 A.M. when it was also struck by a terrifying jolt. Even though the sea appeared as smooth as "mirror glass," the *Wellington*'s captain reported in his log, the heavy ship "shivered and shook like a springless wagon on a corduroy road."

Meanwhile, at Ocean Beach on the city of San Francisco's southwestern fringes, a local laborer named Clarence Judson had just entered the frigid waters of the Pacific for a bracing, early morning swim before heading off to work. A few yards from shore, and possibly no more than five miles from the earthquake's epicenter, Judson was abruptly knocked down "to his knees" by a powerful shock, he later recalled:

> I got up and was down again. I was dazed and stunned,
> and being tossed about by the breakers, my ears full of

salt water and about a gallon in my stomach. I was thrown down three times, and only by desperate fighting did I get out [of the water] at all. . . .

I tried to run to where my shoes, hat and bathrobe lay, but I guess I must have described all kinds of figures in the sand. I thought I was paralyzed. Then I thought of lightning, as the beach was full of phosphorescence. Every step I took left a brilliant iridescent streak. I jumped on my bathrobe to save me.

"WE'RE GOING INTO THE BAY!": THE CITY IS STRUCK

Some eight or nine miles northeast of Ocean Beach, police sergeant Jesse Cook was making his usual early morning rounds through San Francisco's produce district, the one part of the city that was already buzzing with activity just after 5:00 A.M. His shift nearly over, Cook had just stopped to chat with a vegetable seller on hilly Washington Street before heading for the police station to clock out. Suddenly, he heard the deep rumble of giant breakers crashing against a cliff. Turning away from the vendor, Cook instinctively gazed westward down Washington Street toward the distant Pacific. To his horror, he saw the road before him rising and falling, rising and falling, like the sea. "The whole street was undulating. It was as if the waves of the ocean were coming toward me, billowing as they came," he would remember.

As the ominous waves moved closer, Cook noticed the shops and warehouses that lined Washington Street on either side begin to sway crazily. Soon a dangerous cascade of bricks, stone, and broken glass was raining down on the sidewalks and roadway. Desperate to escape the avalanche of debris, Cook half ran, half staggered onto adjoining Davis Street. Immediately, he regretted his decision. "Davis Street split right open in front of me," the policeman later recalled. "A gaping trench. . . about six feet deep and half full of water suddenly

As the earthquake rippled through San Francisco, entire streets were torn apart by the strong vibrations. Cable car tracks and cobblestones were wrenched apart *(above)*, and gaping holes in the street proved hazardous to those trying to evacuate the city.

yawned and sprang up on the sidewalk at the southeast corner while the walls of the building I had marked for my asylum began tottering. Before I could get into the shelter of the doorway those walls had actually fallen inward. But the stacked-up cases of produce that filled the place prevented them from wholly collapsing."

Yet Cook's nightmare was not over. After a respite of no more than ten seconds from the vicious shaking, another shock hit. Although shorter in duration than the first shock—perhaps 20 seconds as opposed to 40—this one proved to be even more intense. "The ground," Cook later declared, "seemed to twist . . . like a top while it jerked this way and that, and up and down and every way." Turning to a man huddled next to him in the warehouse doorway the police officer blurted out: "My God, we're going into the bay!"

"I THOUGHT THE END OF THE WORLD HAD COME"

Unlike police sergeant Cook and the vendors and other workers in the produce district, most of San Francisco's citizens were still in bed at 5:12 A.M. when the earthquake struck. Many died in their beds as scores of flimsily constructed hotels, boardinghouses, and single-family dwellings suddenly disappeared into heaps of splintered wood and shattered brick in the first seconds of violent shaking.

Those who could escape their homes and lodging places poured onto the streets, many still dressed in their night-clothes. There, they were often exposed to new dangers from falling masonry, as G.A. Raymond, a businessman staying at the Palace Hotel on heavily built up Market Street, quickly discovered. "I awoke as I was thrown out of bed," Raymond later recalled of that deadly morning:

> I grabbed my clothing and rushed down into the [hotel] office, where dozens were already congregated. Suddenly the lights went out, and every one rushed for the door.
>
> Outside I witnessed a sight I never want to see again. It was dawn and light. I looked up. The air was filled with falling stones. People around me were crushed to death on all sides. All around the huge buildings were shaking and waving. . . .
>
> I asked a man standing next to me what happened. Before he could answer a thousand bricks fell on him and he was killed. A woman threw her arms around my neck. I pushed her away and fled. All around me buildings were rocking. . . . As I ran people on all sides were crying, praying and calling for help. I thought the end of the world had come. . . .
>
> At places the streets had cracked and opened. Chasms extended in all directions. . . . I was crazy with fear and the horrible sights. . . .

"A Sickening, Dreadful Swaying of the Earth"

John Barrett, an editor for the San Francisco newspaper the *Examiner*, had just finished a long night of work and was standing outside his downtown office chatting with several coworkers when the temblor struck. Suddenly, Barrett and his companions found themselves staggering and reeling. His eyewitness account of the earthquake makes for compelling reading:

> It was as if the earth was slipping gently from under our feet. Then came a sickening swaying of the earth that threw us flat upon our faces. We struggled in the street. We could not get on our feet.
>
> I looked in a dazed fashion around me. I saw for an instant the big buildings in what looked like a crazy dance. Then it seemed as though my head were split with the roar that crashed into my ears. Big buildings were crumbling

THE PERILS OF "MADE LAND"

Despite the horrors that G.A. Raymond witnessed in the heart of the downtown district, the earthquake actually took its greatest toll elsewhere in San Francisco, in those areas of the city that had been constructed on so-called made land. By the term *made land*, San Franciscans meant those marshlands, underground creeks, and sections of San Francisco Bay that had been filled in during the Gold Rush era to create new residential and commercial areas for the rapidly growing metropolis. San Francisco's made ground was typically an unstable hodgepodge of loose soil, sand, rocks, rotting timber, and other as one might crush a biscuit in one's hand. Great gray clouds of dust shot up with flying timbers, and storms of masonry rained into the street. Wild, high jangles of smashing glass cut a sharp note into the frightful roaring. Ahead of me a great cornice crushed a man as if he were a maggot. . . .

Everywhere men were on all fours in the street, like crawling bugs. Still the sickening, dreadful swaying of the earth continued. . . . I saw trolley tracks uprooted, twisted fantastically. I saw wide wounds in the street. Water flooded out of one. A deadly odor of gas from a broken main swept out of the other. Telegraph poles were rocked like matches. A wild tangle of wires was in the street. Some of the wires wriggled and shot blue sparks.

From the south of us, faint, but all too clear, came a horrible chorus of human cries of agony. Down there in a ramshackle section of the city the wretched houses had fallen in upon the sleeping families. . . .

debris. In a process that scientists refer to as soil liquefaction, powerful earthquake waves can swiftly reduce the firmness and strength of made land, leaving the shaken soil with the consistency of a soft pudding or jelly.

In 1906, one of the most densely populated areas in all of San Francisco was constructed largely on made land: the South of the Slot district. Many of the rickety wooden-frame cottages and boardinghouses that crammed the streets of the working-class neighborhoods to the south of Market Street rested on what had been a huge swamp a few decades earlier. Dozens of these flimsy dwellings came crashing down as the ground beneath them liquefied during the terrible shaking and wrenching of the quake. Hundreds—perhaps thousands—of residents were killed instantly while hundreds more were buried alive under mountains of debris.

The single most deadly collapse of a building on made land during the 1906 earthquake occurred on Valencia Street in the South of the Slot. During the temblor's first seconds, a cheap rooming house known as the Valencia Street Hotel lurched forward violently, then literally sank into the marshy soil on which it had once rested. In an instant, the wooden hotel had shrunk from four stories to just one, trapping most of its occupants underneath the mushy landfill. As many as 200 men, women, and children are believed to have perished in the crumpled building. Adding to the horror, many of the victims

In response to the demand for housing during the Gold Rush, structures were built on unstable fortified marshland. When the great quake pulsed through San Francisco, the land beneath these buildings, such as the Valencia Street Hotel (above), shifted and liquefied. The first three floors of the hotel sank straight down into the ground.

drowned in water gushing in from a nearby burst water main while rescuers could only look on helplessly.

BUILDINGS THAT SURVIVED AND BUILDINGS THAT DID NOT

The composition of the ground beneath San Francisco's thousands of houses and other buildings was of critical importance in determining their ability to withstand the earthquake of 1906. Yet construction techniques and materials also played a vital role in determining whether a building emerged from the earthquake virtually unscathed or severely damaged.

Unfortunately for the inhabitants of San Francisco in 1906, a large number of the city's structures were poorly constructed. According to some estimates, fully 90 percent of the city's buildings had wood frames. A properly constructed wood frame structure on solid ground can actually absorb earthquake shocks quite well. Many of San Francisco's wood houses, however, had been thrown up as quickly and cheaply as possible, and even the relatively well-constructed ones had shoddily made chimneys that toppled and disintegrated during the violent shaking. When these heavy brick columns came crashing down on the houses to which they were attached or on neighboring homes, they usually caused major structural damage, not to mention serious injury to those inside. As G.A. Raymond's and police sergeant Cook's terrifying experiences during the earthquake illustrated, many of the seemingly solid brick buildings that lined the streets of the city's downtown and commercial districts had also been poorly constructed, leaving them with dangerously weak walls that quickly crumbled during the quake.

San Francisco's relatively small number of iron and steel-framed buildings fared the best during the earthquake. Probably the most well-constructed, metal-framed structure in early twentieth-century San Francisco was also the city's most beloved landmark: the luxurious, 755-room Palace Hotel on Market Street. Although the hotel rocked back and forth during the temblor with sufficient violence to propel some guests like G.A. Raymond right out of their beds, the elegant, seven-story building emerged from the earthquake with only minor damage. This had everything to do with the Palace's wealthy creator, San Francisco banker William Ralston. When he decided to build the hotel during the early 1870s, the two earthquakes that had struck San Francisco in 1865 and 1868 were very much on Ralston's mind. Although the temblors were significantly weaker than the quake that would ravish San Francisco in April 1906, they had still caused thousands of dollars in damage to the city's buildings. To provide his new hotel with as much stability and strength as possible in the event of another earthquake, Ralston built it on mammoth, 12-foot-deep, pillar foundations and had 3,000 tons of reinforcing iron woven into its 2-foot-thick outer brick walls.

While metal-girded buildings such as the Palace Hotel generally survived the San Francisco earthquake of 1906 virtually intact, one steel-framed structure that failed to withstand the powerful shaking was the recently completed City Hall. Built over a period of more than 20 years at a cost to taxpayers of more than $6 million, in 1906 the San Francisco City Hall—with its 335-foot bronze dome and gigantic stone pillars—was the largest and most ornate municipal building west of the Mississippi. Yet because the building not only rested on former marshland but was also poorly constructed, once the earthquake hit, what had taken more than two decades to erect took less than two minutes to disintegrate into a nearly unrecognizable heap of rubble. Historians agree that graft was the chief reason for the City Hall's extraordinarily bad construction. Eager to line their own pockets with government funds, corrupt officials and contractors clandestinely substituted cheap, inferior materials for more expensive ones, and nowhere was this dishonest and potentially dangerous practice more apparent than in the use of low-grade mortar to

"The Building Was Shaking and Rolling Like a Mad Thing"

At 5:12 A.M. on April 18, 1906, policeman Edmond Parquette had just entered the front office of the Central Emergency Hospital in the basement of the San Francisco City Hall. Later, he recalled his harrowing experience as the huge stone and brick building collapsed around him:

> I was just stepping through the entrance of the office when the whole place began to shake, and in a few seconds the shaking became so severe that I had to hold on to the door to save myself from falling. . . . The building was shaking and rolling like a mad thing. The furniture was rolling and hopping about, the plaster and everything else on top was falling. Then there was the roar of the earthquake itself, and the crashes and shocks and rumblings as we felt the walls and pillars of the City Hall bursting and breaking over our heads. . . .
>
> Even when the quaking and twisting ceased, the lumps of masonry still kept falling; and above all those noises of crashing and thundering of the quake itself and the thuds of the pillars and cornices as they hit the ground, there were the shrieks and yells of the lunatics, and the moans and cries of the other patients. Everybody seemed to be yelling and shrieking at the top of his voice.
>
> Very quickly after the shocks ceased, the dust began to clear away or settle down, and stopped choking me. The cries died down too, though many of the poor creatures kept on shrieking from terror or moaning from hurts and apprehensions. . . .

cement the building's massive walls and pillars. "As with other graft-plagued structures, including the Hall of Justice," noted author Kurzman, "the earthquake shook off the masonry [brick- and stonework] enveloping City Hall's steel framework like the wind shaking leaves off a tree."

SAN FRANCISCO'S NEIGHBORS ON THE MORNING OF APRIL 18, 1906

The earthquake that roared into the City by the Bay at approximately 5:12 A.M. on April 18, 1906, was felt all the way from Coos Bay, Oregon, some 500 miles north of San Francisco, to Los Angeles, nearly 400 miles to its south. To the east, the temblor was felt as far away as central Nevada. Outside of San Francisco, severe damage from the earthquake occurred a little more than 50 miles to the north of the Bay City in Santa Rosa and approximately 45 miles to its south in San Jose. Stanford University in Palo Alto, about 30 miles south of San Francisco, also suffered major damage.

Santa Rosa, largely because of its location in a small basin, or depression, of loose soil that served to amplify the shaking, was particularly hard hit. Scores of wood-frame buildings and just about every brick building in the downtown area collapsed. At least 64 people died in the earthquake and the numerous fires that followed it. The greatest loss of life from the earthquake outside of San Francisco, however, occurred near San Jose at Agnews State Hospital, a 1,000-bed facility for the mentally ill. When the shoddily constructed brick hospital collapsed during the shaking, more than 100 patients and employees were buried in the wreckage, and hundreds of others were seriously injured. Adding to the pandemonium, immediately after the hospital's collapse some of the surviving inmates ran wildly around the hospital grounds "attacking everyone who came in their path," according to one eyewitness. Administrators ended up chaining the hysterical patients to trees until the situation could be brought under control.

Just to the north of San Jose at Stanford University in Palo Alto, damage was also extensive. Fortunately, only one student and one staff member died during the shaking, but fully one-third of the 15-year-old campus was destroyed, including the gymnasium, the chapel, the still unfinished library, the art museum, and the 10-story Memorial Arch that marked the entrance to the Main Quad. Yet even as the rubble was being cleared away from the campus, Stanford professors, working with scientists from other leading California universities, were making vital discoveries regarding the origins and nature of the April 18 disaster, findings that were to revolutionize the young field of earthquake science.

3 Earthquake Science in 1906 and Today

Before the earthquake of April 18, 1906, seismology (the science of earthquakes) received little attention in California and the United States generally, despite the fact that earthquakes occurred regularly along California's long Pacific coastline. Although most of the temblors were mild and did little more than rattle windows or break a few dishes, in 1865 and 1868 the San Francisco Bay Area was struck by two unusually strong earthquakes. Significantly less powerful than the earthquake of 1906, the temblors nonetheless caused chimneys and walls to fall and killed a total of 30 people, about a quarter of them in the city of San Francisco.

On the heels of the 1868 earthquake, the government of San Francisco formed a special committee to investigate the temblor's origins and to discuss how earthquake-related damage might be reduced in the future. The new commission proved short-lived, however. When San Francisco's business leaders got wind of the committee, they immediately pressured the mayor into dissolving it. They argued that the commission would only hurt San Francisco's reputation and economy by calling attention to the recent earthquakes.

Even in other parts of the world where earthquake science was taken more seriously than in the United States, such as in western Europe and Japan, seismology was still very much in its infancy on the eve of the San Francisco earthquake. The first modern seismograph—an instrument that can detect and simultaneously record the seismic waves, or vibrations, from earthquakes as they move through the Earth—had been invented only a decade earlier by an English scientist working in earthquake-prone Japan. The simple machine featured a pendulum with an ink pen that swung against a continuously rotating, paper-covered drum. The shaking of an earthquake caused the pendulum and the cylinder to move relative to each other. As the paper on the drum unrolled, the pen drew

The 10 Highest-Magnitude Earthquakes in World History

1960 Chile, magnitude 9.5
1964 Prince William Sound, Alaska, magnitude 9.2
2004 Sumatra-Andaman Islands, magnitude 9.1
1952 Kamchatka Peninsula, Russia, magnitude 9.0
1700 Cascadia Subduction Zone (off America's Pacific Northwest coast), magnitude 9.0
1906 Off the Coast of Ecuador, magnitude 8.8
1965 Rat Islands, Alaska, magnitude 8.7
1755 Lisbon, Portugal, magnitude 8.7
2005 Northern Sumatra, Indonesia, magnitude 8.6
1957 Andreanof Islands, Alaska, magnitude 8.6

(Source: U.S. Geological Survey)

a jagged line along it, with the zigzags becoming sharper as the vibrations increased. As of April 18, 1906, there were only 96 seismographs in the entire world, and the vast majority of them were thousands of miles away from San Francisco in Asia and Europe. Nonetheless, the earthquake that struck the Bay City at approximately 5:12 A.M. was so violent that virtually every single one of the instruments—from Tokyo and Bombay to Vienna and London—recorded it.

THE EARTHQUAKE INVESTIGATION COMMISSION GOES TO WORK

In the wake of the temblor of April 18, 1906, with much of the city in ruins and untold thousands dead or injured, California's political leadership decided that the time was long overdue to examine how and why earthquakes occurred in the state. Within three days of the devastating quake, Governor George Pardee announced the formation of a new scientific commission to study the causes and impact of the Bay Area disaster. Led by Andrew C. Lawson, the highly respected chairman of the geology department at the University of California at Berkeley, the committee was chiefly composed of Californians, including professors from the Chabot Observatory in Oakland and Stanford University.

The State Earthquake Investigation Commission immediately set out to study the vast swath of land to the north and south of San Francisco that had been affected by the earthquake. As journalist David Perlman wrote in his article "The Great Quake: 1906–2006: Quake Propelled Seismology," to better understand what had happened on the morning of April 18, Lawson's team systematically "studied every crack and sundered ground surface, every report of earth movement up and down the entire rupture zone." Soon their work came to focus on what was then called the San Andreas Rift—later known as the San Andreas Fault—a long break in the Earth's

The 10 Deadliest Earthquakes in the World Since 1900

The deadliest earthquake of all time is thought to have taken place in 1556 in Shaanxi Province, China. An estimated 830,000 people were killed.

2004	Sumatra, Indonesia	283,106	(deaths also from tsunami*)
1976	Tangshan, China	255,000	(official toll; estimated toll up to 655,000)
1927	Qinghai, China	200,000	
1920	Gansu, China	200,000	(many from quake-triggered landslides)
1923	Kanto, Japan	143,000	(most from fires)
1948	Turkmenistan	110,000	
1908	Messina, Italy	70,000 to 100,000	(deaths also from a tsunami)
2005	Pakistan	80,361	
1932	Gansu, China	70,000	
1970	Peru	66,000	(deaths from rockslide, floods)

(Source: U.S. Geological Survey)

* A tsunami is an extremely large ocean wave caused by an underwater earthquake or volcanic eruption.

outer layer that the scientists suspected was linked in some way to the violent shaking.

Lawson had been aware of the San Andreas Fault for several years and had even mapped short sections of it. But not until the commission of 1906 was formed had anyone attempted to trace the entire fault line. For two years, Lawson and his team laboriously followed the rift along ponds and streams and up and down poison oak–covered hills on foot and horseback. In the end, they determined that the San Andreas zone stretched for some 700 miles along California's coastline, covering almost the entire length of the state. During the April 18 earthquake, they further discovered, nearly 300 miles of the Earth's surface along the fault line had ruptured.

THE ELASTIC REBOUND THEORY AND PLATE TECTONICS

As Lawson's team mapped the San Andreas Fault, they were also carefully measuring the land movements on either side of the rupture. By analyzing their data, the scientists were able to determine that the earthquake's vibrations had shifted the ground horizontally instead of vertically, as scientists had previously believed. This finding led team member Henry Fielding Reid, a geology professor at Johns Hopkins University in Maryland, to propose a theory regarding the origin of earthquakes. Later dubbed the "theory of elastic rebound," Reid's hypothesis was to have a revolutionary impact on the young field of seismology.

According to Reid's theory, earthquakes are created by powerful strains that slowly accumulate in rock masses along faults, weak spots in the planet's outer shell. When the stresses become more powerful than the strength of the rocks, the pent-up energy is suddenly released with a jolt as the Earth's brittle shell snaps like a rubber band stretched beyond its breaking point. The place on the fault where this abrupt fracture and release of energy takes place is called the earthquake's focus;

The San Andreas fault was found to be the source of the great earthquake that destroyed so much of San Francisco in 1906. After further investigation, geologists have determined that the entire San Andreas fault system, which includes the main split in the earth along with many other, smaller faults, is more than 800 miles long and at least 10 miles deep.

the point on the Earth's surface directly above it is the earthquake's epicenter.

A century after the 1906 earthquake that inspired his hypothesis, Reid's theory (regarding how built-up energy in the Earth's surface is eventually released on faults) is still considered as the fundamental principle of seismology. Our knowledge regarding the true nature of the Earth's outer layer and geological faults, however, has expanded enormously since Reid's time. Most important for his theory of how earthquakes are born, scientists now know that the Earth's outer shell, or lithosphere, is composed of a number of rigid, continuously moving plates and that faults lie on the boundaries between them. Plates may support oceans, continents, or a combination of both. The big slabs slide slowly over a much hotter, fluidlike layer just beneath the lithosphere called the asthenosphere, often grazing one another like ships passing too closely in the night.

According to the so-called plate tectonic theory that first gained widespread acceptance in the 1960s, earthquakes occur when stresses on the boundaries between two plates reach a critical point and are abruptly released. Scientists discovered that the entire length of California's San Andreas Fault sits on the boundary between two massive plates: the Pacific to the east and the North American to the west. At about 5:12 A.M. on April 18, 1906, seismologists now know, pressure that had accumulated on the San Andreas Fault caused the rocks to suddenly snap somewhere below the ocean floor just west of San Francisco. That snapping released huge amounts of pent-up energy in the form of a series of seismic waves that roared across water and land at speeds of up to 8,000 miles per hour to produce the deadliest earthquake in U.S. history.

OTHER FINDINGS OF THE EARTHQUAKE INVESTIGATION COMMISSION

The mapping of the entire San Andreas Fault in California and Henry Reid's formulation of the elastic rebound theory are generally considered as the two most important contributions of the commission formed by Governor Pardee. A third significant finding of the two-year study of the quake-ravaged area in and around San Francisco was the close relationship between ground composition and the extent of damage to buildings and other structures.

Published in two volumes in 1908 and 1910, the Lawson Report, as the commission's official findings are popularly known, summarized the detailed surveys that team members compiled regarding how well various structures in different locations held up during the earthquake. Team members carefully analyzed the composition of the ground beneath those buildings that received the most damage and those that survived the temblor virtually intact. The commission concluded that the most intense and destructive shaking occurred on soft, loosely compacted soils such as the made land that lay beneath large portions of San Francisco's South of the Slot district. Studies of outlying areas where structural damage was particularly severe also showed that towns in sediment-filled valleys or basins such as Santa Rosa also experienced more violent shaking on the morning of April 18, 1906, than neighboring bedrock areas (areas of unbroken solid rock covered by soil).

Although the Lawson Report's conclusions regarding the link between certain types of ground and more intense and destructive shaking have held up over the decades since its publication, the report's conclusions regarding the probable epicenter of the San Francisco earthquake have not. Because of the relatively crude state of seismographs in 1906, the Earthquake Investigation Commission had to rely primarily on fieldwork to determine just where along the San Andreas Fault the great temblor might have originated. In the village of Olema, about 30 miles northwest of San Francisco in Marin County, team members were amazed to find a fence line that had broken apart during the quake and was now separated by more than 20 feet of ground. Because this was the greatest horizontal displacement of ground that the scientists discovered anywhere along the San Andreas Fault, they assumed that the quake's epicenter was in the little community of Olema.

Today, seismologists know that the earthquake's epicenter was actually in the Pacific Ocean, somewhere to the west of the San Francisco Peninsula. Although scientists disagree regarding the precise location of the quake's offshore birthplace, based in part on meticulous analysis of data from more

The Nine Highest-Magnitude Earthquakes in the United States

1964 Prince William Sound, Alaska, magnitude 9.2

1700 Cascadia Subduction Zone (off the Pacific Northwest Coast), magnitude 9.0

1965 Rat Islands, Alaska, magnitude 8.7

1957 Andreanof Islands, Alaska, magnitude 8.6

1938 Shumagin Islands, Alaska, magnitude 8.2

1946 Unimak Island, Alaska, magnitude 8.1

1811 New Madrid Region, Territory of Missouri, magnitude 8.1

1899 Yakutat Bay, Alaska, magnitude 8.0

1812 New Madrid Region, Territory of Missouri, magnitude 8.0

(Source: U.S. Geological Survey)

recent earthquakes on the San Andreas Fault, many leading experts now place the epicenter one or two miles off the shore of Golden Gate Park.

DETERMINING THE SEVERITY OF THE 1906 EARTHQUAKE: INTENSITY

The severity of an earthquake may be expressed both in terms of intensity and of magnitude. The two ways to rank earthquakes are very different. Intensity, the actual impact of the shaking on an area's buildings, natural features, and human inhabitants, is based on personal observations, while magnitude, a mathematical measurement of the amount of energy released at an earthquake's source, is based on instrumental records. In 1906, scientists relied on intensity, which varies from one part of the affected region to another depending on the observer's distance from the epicenter and the type of ground—soft, loose soil or solid bedrock—underlying the area, to assess an earthquake's severity.

During the late nineteenth century, scientists around the world developed different scales to measure earthquake intensity. As of 1906, the most commonly used scale was the Rossi-Forel, named for its two European creators, Michele de Rossi and François Forel. It classified earthquakes on a scale of 1 to 10, with 10 having the greatest intensity. According to the Rossi-Forel Scale, the San Francisco quake had a value of 9, an earthquake that causes some buildings to collapse entirely and topples chimneys and walls. That made the 1906 temblor just one step down from a number 10 earthquake, a catastrophic seismic event described on the Rossi-Forel Scale as causing "great disasters, ruins, [and] . . . rock falls from mountains."

The Italian scientist Giuseppe Mercalli refined the Rossi-Forel Scale in an attempt to make its rather vague descriptions more precise during the early 1900s. Today, a modified version of Mercalli's scale known as the Modified Mercalli Intensity Scale (abbreviated as MM) is the most widely used intensity scale in the United States. Designated by Roman numerals, its 12 ascending levels of intensity range from barely noticeable shaking to full-scale destruction and are specifically adopted for North American conditions. According to the Modified Mercalli Scale, the 1906 earthquake reached a Level VIII, or "Destructive," intensity in the city of San Francisco and a Level IX to the north in Santa Rosa, whose downtown area was virtually leveled on April 18. Level VIII is characterized by the falling of chimneys, walls, columns, and monuments; the total collapse of poorly constructed buildings; and only slight damage to specially designed structures such as San Francisco's iron-corseted Palace Hotel. Level IX is characterized by severe damage to well-constructed, substantial buildings; considerable damage

Top Ten Deaths in the United States from Earthquakes

Year	Location	Deaths	Notes
1906	San Francisco, California	about 3,000	(many deaths also from fires)
1946	Aleutian Islands, Alaska	165	(most deaths from a tsunami in Hawaii)
1964	Prince William Sound, Alaska	125	(most deaths from a tsunami)
1933	Long Beach, California	115	(many from quake-triggered landslides)
1868	Hawaii Island, Hawaii	77	(deaths from a tsunami and landslides)
1971	San Fernando, California	65	
1989	Santa Cruz County, California	63	
1960	Hawaii	61	(caused by an earthquake and tsunami in Chile)
1994	Northridge, California	60	
1886	Charleston, South Carolina	60	

(Source: U.S. Geological Survey)

to structures specially designed to withstand intense shaking; and buildings shifted off their foundations.

MEASURING THE MAGNITUDE OF THE SAN FRANCISCO EARTHQUAKE

In 1906, scientists could only rate the severity of the San Francisco earthquake in terms of intensity. The earthquake's magnitude—the amount of energy released into the ground at the temblor's origin or focus—could not be determined because seismographs were not yet sophisticated enough to accurately measure it. Nor had a scale to assess varying levels of magnitude with any mathematical precision been developed at the time of the San Francisco quake. When such a scale was finally created by Charles Richter of the California Institute of Technology in 1935, seismologists used it to analyze written records or seismograms from U.S., European, and Asian seismographs that had picked up the shaking in California on the morning of April 18, 1906.

On his scale, Richter expressed magnitude in whole numbers and decimal fractions. "Moderate" earthquakes causing only slight damage to most structures were assigned magnitudes of between 5.0 and 5.9, while "great" earthquakes capable of causing severe and widespread damage and loss of life in populated areas several hundred miles across were assigned magnitudes of 8.0 and above. During the mid-twentieth century, scientists assigned the San Francisco earthquake a magnitude of 8.3 on the new Richter scale, even though the relatively primitive seismographs in use in 1906 made it difficult to assess the quake's magnitude with any real precision.

Since the late twentieth century, scientists have largely replaced the Richter scale with other, more accurate ways of measuring the energy released by earthquakes, particularly the Moment Magnitude Scale introduced in 1979 by seismologists Hiroo Kanamori of the California Institute of Technology and Tom Hanks of the U.S. Geological Survey.

Seismologist Charles Francis Richter *(above)* developed a measurement system for earthquakes. Using data from a seismograph, the Richter scale calculates the magnitude of any earthquake and has no upper limit.

Two recent studies, one using data from ground displacements during the earthquake and another based on measurements recorded at nearly 100 seismograph stations around the globe on April 18, 1906, have assigned a magnitude of between 7.7 and 7.9 on the Moment Magnitude Scale to the San Francisco earthquake.

At a magnitude of 9.2, the earthquake at Prince William Sound, Alaska, on March, 27, 1964, was the most powerful earthquake in the United States and the second strongest in world history (after a 9.5 magnitude earthquake in Chile in 1960). Yet, because it occurred in a relatively unpopulated area, the Alaska quake claimed just 125 lives. In sharp contrast, in San Francisco a high population density combined with poor ground composition and building construction and extensive post-earthquake fires resulted in perhaps 300 times as many deaths. Thus, even though the temblor of April 18, 1906, released only half as much energy as the one at Prince William Sound, more than a century later, the San Francisco earthquake remains far and away the deadliest quake in U.S. history.

4. San Francisco in Flames

A t 5:12 A.M. on Wednesday, April 18, 1906, San Francisco fire chief Dennis Sullivan was asleep in bed on the top floor of the Bush Street fire station, where he and his wife, Margaret, made their home. When the first great shock hit, Sullivan leapt out of bed to check on Margaret in the adjoining room. Suddenly, a wall and massive cupola from the five-story hotel next door toppled and crashed down on the fire station's roof. Carried along by an avalanche of bricks and debris, the Sullivans plunged down three stories to the engine house cellar. Margaret Sullivan survived, but her husband's skull was fractured and his entire body scalded by steam from a broken boiler, a big tank in which water is heated and stored. Sullivan would die three days later, never having regained consciousness.

THE SAN FRANCISCO FIRE DEPARTMENT MAKES A TERRIBLE DISCOVERY

While San Francisco's top firefighter lay mortally wounded in the Bush Street fire station, ruptured gas mains, crossed electrical wires, and overturned wood stoves and kerosene lamps were sparking dozens of fires all over the stricken city.

54

Yet not one of the city's many fire alarms rang on the morning of April 18: The violent shaking had made a shambles of the fire department's central dispatching office in Chinatown. Six hundred glass jars stored on several long shelves held the wet-cell batteries that powered San Francisco's extensive alarm system. During the first seconds of the temblor, all but 40 of the jars toppled to the floor and shattered.

With columns of black smoke curling into the sky from the more than 50 blazes already burning within minutes of the quake, San Francisco's firefighters hardly needed alarms to alert them to the growing conflagration, however. All across the city, fire crews dashed for the nearest water hydrants. But when they attached their hoses to the cast-iron hydrants and turned the valves, the men made a terrible discovery. There was no water.

Although the firefighters could not have realized it then, powerful seismic waves had fractured thousands of the underground iron pipes that connected the hydrants with distant reservoirs, and some 80 million gallons of precious water was now spewing out of the cracked conduits into the soil. As the firefighters desperately tried to pump wastewater from the city's sewers, the fires—fed by debris and fanned by hot, dry winds from the northeast—continued to spread, particularly in the crowded South of the Slot district, an area that had already suffered severe earthquake damage.

THREE GREAT FIRES DEVELOP TO THE SOUTH AND NORTH OF MARKET STREET

By midmorning, isolated fires in the cheap rooming houses, warehouses, and other rickety wooden structures that packed the quake-ravaged South of the Slot were starting to merge into panic-inducing curtains of flame. "Residents terrified and stunned by the collapse of their homes and hotels, stood helpless out in the streets," wrote Simon Winchester in *A Crack in the Edge of the World: American and the Great California Earthquake of 1906*: "Then, as the fires came, they scattered and began to flee, not knowing which way to run to avoid being trapped by a wall of flame." On Mission Street, a Catholic priest, Father Ralph Hunt, saw several people frantically trying to unbury a man pinned under debris from a fallen building as the inferno closed in on them. "Don't leave me here to die like this," Hunt remembered the man pleading over and over again. Finally, when it was apparent that nothing more could be done for the man, one of the would-be rescuers knelt down on the ground next to him. After speaking quietly with the victim for several minutes, the fellow rose to his feet, pulled a revolver from his

After the earthquake and its aftershocks came and went, the dazed citizens walked from the rubble of their homes into the streets. When it became clear that the city was on fire, most abandoned their possessions and the remains of their homes to find safety and shelter.

pocket, and fired it directly into the trapped man's head, killing him instantly.

Fires began breaking out to the north as well as the south of Market Street immediately following the temblor, especially in the bustling wholesale district near the waterfront. Since this area contained more brick structures than South of the Slot, however, the fires moved more slowly than on the opposite side of Market Street. Nonetheless, the blazes advanced steadily southward and westward during the hours after the quake, edging ever closer to Market Street itself and the heart of San Francisco's downtown district.

Around 10:00 A.M., the situation to the north of Market Street took a decided turn for the worse when a big fire broke out in the Hayes Valley section several blocks west of City Hall. According to tradition, the blaze began when a woman on Hayes Street, unaware that her chimney had been damaged during the quake, lit her woodstove to cook a ham and eggs breakfast and set her entire house on fire. Merging with other lesser blazes, the so-called Ham and Eggs Fire raced from house to house, street to street, carried along by a stiff wind blowing in from the bay.

GENERAL FUNSTON AND MAYOR SCHMITZ TAKE CHARGE

At 5:12 A.M., Brigadier General Frederick Funston, a highly decorated veteran of the Spanish-American War and the acting commander of the U.S. Army's Pacific Division, was awakened by a powerful jolt. Rushing out of his home on Russian Hill, Funston gazed down at the city below and immediately noticed smoke rising into the sky from the fires that were already erupting in the wholesale district. Many of the underground water lines to the city's hydrants, the general quickly surmised, must have broken during the intense shaking, and San Francisco's firefighters, police, and ambulance squads would soon face overwhelming challenges. Fearing the city was on the brink of complete chaos, Funston felt he had no choice but to take immediate and drastic action: He decided to call out the troops.

In 1906, the San Francisco Peninsula was home to two U.S. Army bases, the Presidio near Golden Gate Park (the Pacific Division's headquarters) and Fort Mason on San Francisco Bay. Since the quake had knocked out all telephone communication in the city, Funston fired off written messages to the bases' commanders ordering them to rush all available troops to the Hall of Justice to report to Mayor Schmitz and police chief Jeremiah Dinan. (Funston did not direct the soldiers to City Hall because a policeman had already told him about its spectacular collapse.) By 8:00 A.M., 1,000 rifle-toting troops had arrived at the Hall of Justice near Portsmouth Square ready to place themselves at the disposal of the mayor and police chief.

Like Funston, Mayor Schmitz worried that the city would slide into anarchy unless aggressive and prompt action was taken. Somewhat ironically, in light of the mayor's own reputation for graft, Schmitz's chief concern seemed to be with looting. Grimly determined to head off any looting of damaged stores and other businesses, Schmitz issued one of the most controversial anticrime measures in American history. Although the mayor had no legal right to make such a bold pronouncement, his measure authorized the army, police, state militia, and specially deputized civilian volunteers to shoot suspected looters on the spot. Later in the day, Schmitz amended the measure to allow authorities to kill "any and all persons" suspected of any crime and had thousands of copies of his draconian proclamation posted throughout the city.

Schmitz's other actions during the first hours after the earthquake were considerably less controversial than his infamous "shoot-to-kill" order. He directed local electrical and gas companies to suspend services until further notification, warned citizens regarding fire hazards from leaking gas pipes and broken chimneys, banned the sale of alcohol, and declared an overnight curfew throughout the city. Schmitz also announced that he was forming a committee of 50 respected San Francisco business and community leaders to help him govern the devastated metropolis. As chairman of the new "Committee of Fifty," Schmitz appointed (no doubt to the surprise of many) former San Francisco mayor James D. Phelan, a zealous political reformer and one of his harshest critics. He also asked another influential opponent of his administration, the wealthy political reformer Rudolph Spreckels to join the committee. Just one day after learning that he and his crony, Abe Ruef, were the targets of a major corruption investigation, Schmitz appeared determined to use the unexpected disaster that had struck San Francisco as an opportunity to prove his basic integrity and win over his detractors.

THE DECISION TO USE EXPLOSIVES

Fortunately, the military's telegraph system was still functioning after the earthquake, and Funston and Schmitz fired off cables to Washington, D.C., and Sacramento (California's capital) asking for tents, food, medicine, hoses, fire engines, and dynamite. Funston and Schmitz's request for dynamite might seem odd. Yet as the blazes to the south and north of Market Street continued to spread and the scope of the damage to the city's water distribution system became clearer, both men had begun to pin their hopes for saving San Francisco on explosives.

As former New York City firefighter and author Dennis Smith pointed out in his book *San Francisco Is Burning*, "Three things are required for a fire: fuel, oxygen, and heat." Firefighters extinguish most large blazes by spraying them with water to reduce their heat. In the absence of an adequate water supply, however, they may attempt to extinguish a fire by

PROCLAMATION
BY THE MAYOR

The Federal Troops, the members of the Regular Police Force, and all Special Police Officers have been authorized to KILL any and all persons found engaged in looting or in the commission of any other crime.

I have directed all the Gas and Electric Lighting Companies not to turn on Gas or Electricity until I order them to do so; you may therefor expect the city to remain in darkness for an indefinite time.

I request all citizens to remain at home from darkness until daylight of every night until order is restored.

I Warn all citizens of the danger of fire from damaged or destroyed chimneys, broken or leaking gas pipes or fixtures, or any like cause.

E. E. SCHMITZ, Mayor.
Dated, April 18, 1906.

ALTVATER PRINT, MISSION AND 220 STS

With no prior experience in handling an earthquake disaster, the mayor of San Francisco was afraid that looting would spiral into anarchy and widespread crime. In an unprecedented move, he allowed the army, the police, state-run militia, and volunteers to shoot those they suspected of committing a crime.

destroying its fuel, typically by blowing up exposed structures in the fire's path to create an empty space that the flames cannot cross. This man-made wasteland is called a firebreak.

Although he had grave reservations regarding the potential hazards of the scheme, San Francisco's newly appointed acting fire chief, 68-year-old John Dougherty, agreed to go along with the general and mayor's plan to fight the growing conflagration with explosives. Dougherty knew that his longtime boss, Dennis Sullivan, viewed dynamite as a potential tool for controlling major blazes, even though the San Francisco Fire Department had never had a chance to try it out in a fire. Recently, Sullivan had begun pestering City Hall for funds to purchase dynamite sticks and provide training for his crews in how to safely use them to create firebreaks. Yet Sullivan was no more successful in wresting money from the mayor and his cronies for this project than he had been for expansion of the fire department's water supply.

Around midmorning, using dynamite and other explosives sent over from the Presidio military base, firefighters and army troops began blowing up buildings in the path of what would become known as the "South of Market Fire." Despite the fact that neither the firemen nor the soldiers had any training in creating firebreaks with explosives, Schmitz and Funston were optimistic regarding the effectiveness of the new firefighting strategy. Over the course of the next few days, it would become painfully clear just how misplaced their faith in these untrained demolition crews was.

TWO SAN FRANCISCO LANDMARKS GO UP IN FLAMES

All morning, the San Francisco Fire Department, aided by volunteer civilian firefighters, had struggled heroically to keep the raging infernos in South of the Slot from reaching the city's downtown district. Nonetheless, by noon several buildings on the south side of Market Street, San Francisco's main business thoroughfare, were burning, including the city's tallest building and one of its most famous landmarks: the 16-story Call Building at the corner of Market and Third Street.

Built not quite a decade before, the steel-framed Call Building had survived the violent shaking the morning of April 18 with only minor damage. But within a few hours of the earthquake, out-of-control blazes in the South of the Slot had merged into a firestorm that raged up Third Street straight toward the skyscraper like a funnel cloud. Firestorms are formed when a several smaller fires join together into one large fire. As the fires unite, they generate their own winds: powerful, superheated pockets of air that may reach speeds of over 100 miles per hour. Flames from the inferno somehow got into the Call Building's

"The Fire Was Worse Than the Earthquake"

On May 24, 1906, about a month after the great earthquake and fire, San Francisco resident Nellie Keohane wrote a letter to a friend describing her experiences during the disaster. Excerpts from the letter are printed below:

I would have wrote before now but I got a bad cold and was in bed for two weeks . . . but I am much better and was out yesterday for the first time since the earthquake and went around to see the city but I don't want to go again as it is something dreadful to see. We thought the [Mission District] here was bad but to go downtown there is no town there only bricks and iron pipes. . . . I don't think there was ever in the world such misery and worse looking city as this. . . . The [Mission] got the worst of the earthquake as the ground elevator shaft (one of the very few in San Francisco at that time) and were swiftly sucked up to its stately dome, more than 300 feet above street level. "Soon," wrote San Francisco newspaperman James Hopper, "the tallest skyscraper in the city was glowing like a phosphorescent worm. Cataracts [waterfalls] of pulverized fire poured out of its thousand windows."

A short distance east of the Call Building on Market Street stood another San Francisco landmark: the sumptuous, 755-room Palace Hotel. William Ralston, the Palace's builder, had spared no expense in making his showcase hotel not only as earthquake resistant but also as fireproof as possible. Accordingly, the sevenstory Palace has its very own 700,000-gallon water supply for

around here is made ground and there was a creek running through here at one time. [On] the block below me between 17 and 18 and the next street . . . the sidewalks went down six feet and the water and gass pipes were all toren up and twisted in places the houses were thrown on there backs or sides and the people had to be dug out as they were pinned in and lots of them killed and then the fire was worse than the earthquake. . . . The day of the 18th we were on the street all day and night watching the fire and afraid to go in the house. . . . My husband came home and told us we better to the hills or some place of safety, that the fire was coming up fast and should be upon us soon, so we left the place at six in the evening and the house burnt down after twelve at night. We camped out there for a week and could look at the city all in one mass of fire and see where I lived burnt. We could not come in as the streets was so hot you could not stand the heat. . . .

dousing fires and a water distribution system that featured some 25,000 feet of piping and 20,000 feet of fire hose.

Despite Ralston's expensive fireproofing measures and the heroic efforts of firefighters and hotel employees, the Palace could not be saved. When the hotel burst into flame after sparks from a neighboring building rained down on its roof, the Palace's private supply of water, some of which had already been used to battle other Market Street fires, ran out quickly. By early afternoon, the hotel's once magnificent interior had been completely gutted, and a second beloved San Francisco landmark had been lost.

THE BATTLE TO SAVE THE U.S. MINT AND A NEW FIRE

While the Call Building and the Palace Hotel were succumbing to fire, one block from Market at Fifth and Mission Streets another key San Francisco building, the United States Mint, was also in grave danger of being incinerated. In 1906, the three-story granite building was one of the largest mints in the world. Within its massive vaults was stored more than $100 million in silver and $200 million in gold, the equivalent of about $6 billion in today's dollars. Unquestionably, the loss of the mint and its precious gold and silver supplies would be a severe blow for the U.S. economy.

As fires approached from several different directions, 50 mint employees and about a dozen soldiers (sent by General Funston to guard the building against looters) formed themselves into a makeshift fire crew. Fortunately for them, the mint's courtyard had a deep-drilled well, and just 10 days before the earthquake, internal fire hoses had been installed all around the building. When the firestorm arrived, squads stationed on each of the mint's floors and roof immediately began to douse the building with well water. For five hours, the men bravely fought back against a fire so intense that it melted the glass in the mint's windows. At around 5:00 P.M., aided by a sudden shift in the wind, the mint's tireless defenders at last claimed victory over the flames.

In the meantime, several miles west of the U.S. Mint, the Ham and Eggs Fire had devoured the ruins of City Hall, and to the north and east, the so-called North of Market fire was sweeping through the crowded slums of Chinatown and heading toward wealthy Nob Hill. By late evening, the distance between the great conflagrations that had developed during the first hours after the earthquake—the South of Market, North of Market, and Ham and Eggs Fires—had been bridged. Three fires had become one raging inferno with temperatures upward of 2,000°F and the ability to ignite structures more than 100 feet away. A half century after the disaster, photographer Moshe Cohen still vividly remembered what it was like to live through the San Francisco firestorms: "There was just flame and noise and hell. . . . And not just ordinary flames, but whole waves of orange and red and purple and yellow, all mixed up together with a terrible dense smoke that seemed to boil up inside the buildings and then spout upwards. . . ."

Around midnight, just when it seemed that things could not get any worse, a fourth blaze, which had broken out a few hours earlier north of Market Street near Union Square, joined with the others to create the largest and most destructive ocean of flame thus far. "Wednesday night saw the destruction of the very heart of the city," wrote Jack London, who was covering the earthquake and fire for *Collier's* magazine: "There was no withstanding the onrush of the flames. . . ."

5 The Battle for San Francisco Continues

Most of San Francisco's downtown area was a burned-out wasteland by dawn Thursday, and firefighters had shifted their attention to stopping the fire's advance into other parts of the city. Of particular concern to San Francisco's political leadership and fire department was the Western Addition, a large middle-class neighborhood just west of the city's main north-south thoroughfare, Van Ness Avenue. By midmorning, the city's two ranking fire chiefs, John Dougherty and Patrick Shaughnessy; Mayor Schmitz; and the Committee of Fifty had agreed that halting the westward march of the conflagration at Van Ness was now the fire department's top priority.

HOLDING THE LINE AT VAN NESS AVENUE

Van Ness Avenue, which stretched from Market Street in the south all the way to Fort Mason and San Francisco Bay in the north, was a natural place for the fire department to make a stand. Not only did the boulevard border the heavily built-up Western Addition, but it was also unusually wide. At 125 feet across, Van Ness Avenue had great potential as a natural firebreak.

As was true in most parts of the city, none of the freshwater hydrants in the immediate vicinity of the avenue were functioning. Grimly determined to save the hundreds of homes in the Western Addition, firefighters laboriously pulled a hose line along Van Ness all the way from San Francisco Bay to Sacramento Street. At a distance of over a mile, it was "perhaps the longest hose stretch in firefighting history," wrote Dennis Smith in *San Francisco Is Burning.* Despite the fire crew's heroic efforts in bringing saltwater to the heart of Van Ness Avenue, however, by Friday morning, April 20, a decision had been made to use even more desperate measures to ensure that

While the use of dynamite to create firebreaks encouraged the flames instead of extinguishing them, some houses were saved from both the quake and the fire. The stately mansions above stand undamaged amid the rubble of the affected homes.

the approaching flames did not cross the thoroughfare: City officials ordered army troops and firefighters to dynamite 14 blocks along the eastern side of Van Ness, from Union Street southward to Geary. By blowing up all the buildings on this long stretch of the boulevard and then setting backfires to eat up the debris, they hoped to create a firebreak so wide that no

"The Story of an Eyewitness" by Jack London

On the afternoon of Wednesday, April 18, 1906, writer Jack London arrived in San Francisco from his home near Santa Rosa to report on the earthquake and fire for *Collier's* magazine. His long article on the disaster, "The Story of an Eyewitness," was printed in the May 5, 1906, edition of *Collier's*. Excerpts from the story appear below:

Not in history has a modern imperial city been so completely destroyed. San Francisco is gone. Nothing remains of it but memories and a fringe of dwelling-houses on its outskirts. Its industrial section is wiped out. Its business section is wiped out. Its social and residential section is wiped out. The factories and warehouses, the great stores and newspaper buildings, the hotels and the palaces of the nabobs, are all gone. . . .

Within an hour after the earthquake shock the smoke of San Francisco's burning was a lurid tower visible a hundred miles away. And for three days and nights this lurid tower swayed in the sky, reddening the sun, darkening the day, and filling the land with smoke.

flames could possibly jump it. (A backfire is a small fire deliberately started in the path of a large oncoming fire in order to take away its fuel.)

The plan to demolish the buildings on the eastern side of Van Ness Avenue had originated with General Funston and was a strategy that the mayor agreed to only with great reluctance.

On Wednesday morning at a quarter past five came the earthquake. A minute later the flames were leaping upward. In a dozen different quarters south of Market Street, in the working-class ghetto, and in the factories, fires started. There was no opposing the flames. There was no organization, no communication. . . . The telephone and telegraph systems were disrupted. And the great water-mains had burst. . . .

By Wednesday afternoon, inside of twelve hours, half the heart of the city was gone. At that time I watched the vast conflagration from out on the bay. It was dead calm. Not a flicker of wind stirred. Yet from every side wind was pouring in upon the city. East, west, north, and south, strong winds were blowing upon the doomed city. The heated air rising made an enormous suck. Thus did the fire of itself build its own colossal chimney through the atmosphere. Day and night this dead calm continued, and yet, near to the flames, the wind was often half a gale, so mighty was the suck. . . .

An enumeration of the buildings destroyed would be a directory of San Francisco. An enumeration of the buildings undestroyed would be a line and several addresses. An enumeration of the deeds of heroism would stock a library and bankrupt the Carnegie medal fund. An enumeration of the dead—will never be made. All vestiges of them were destroyed by the flames. . . .

One reason for Schmitz's misgivings may have been his fear of angering the many wealthy and powerful San Francisco families who owned homes along the blocks slated for destruction. The mayor's hesitancy to employ explosives at Van Ness was also based on very real concerns regarding their effectiveness as firefighting tools, however. Over the past two days, demolition crews had used dozens of crates of stick dynamite and kegs of black powder (gunpowder) to blow up structures north and south of Market Street. Yet far from helping to contain the blazes, the teams, most of which were composed of soldiers and firemen with little training in the use of explosives, actually seemed to be spreading the fire. Inexperienced crews did the most harm with black powder, a highly incendiary substance more appropriate for blasting mines than leveling buildings. Instead of bringing a building to the ground, black powder typically turned it into a giant Roman candle, as the highly flammable explosive quickly ignited floors, beams, and other woodwork and then sent the burning debris raining down on nearby structures.

Despite the mayor's misgivings, however, by Friday afternoon army troops were using dynamite, black powder, and even field artillery to destroy block upon block of houses and other structures along the east side of Van Ness in accordance with Funston's plan. At one point, the demolition crews decided to blow up the big Viavi Company Complex at Van Ness and Green Street. This proved to be a costly mistake, as the explosion sent large amounts of burning wood hurtling eastward through the air, sparking new fires in the heavily populated Russian Hill and North Beach districts.

Yet, if the Van Ness demolition teams' sometimes clumsy efforts resulted in spreading the fire into new areas to the east, by Friday evening the westward advance of the fire had finally been checked. Because it oversaw the blasting, the army later claimed responsibility for saving the Western Addition. Some civilian eyewitnesses that day remembered things differently, however. It was not the dynamiting, they maintained, but rather a sudden shift in the direction of the wind during the afternoon that pushed the flames back from the western side of Van Ness Avenue.

THE BATTLES FOR MISSION DELORES AND RUSSIAN HILL

With the Van Ness situation now under control, the fire department focused its attention on the Mission District in the southwestern part of the city, an area that had already suffered extensive fire damage. All through Friday night, firefighters and civilian volunteers beat back flames from the still intact western and southern sections of the district with anything they could get their hands on, including brooms, mops, and gunnysacks. Then, during the early hours of Saturday morning, a volunteer stumbled on a working fire hydrant near Mission Delores, the eighteenth-century Spanish mission for which the district had been named. There was just one problem, however: To reach the hydrant and its precious water, the firefighters would somehow have to get their steam engine up an extremely steep slope. Realizing that the fire horses would never be able to handle the climb, the already exhausted firemen began pulling and pushing the heavy engine up the hill themselves. Dozens of civilian onlookers quickly offered to lend a hand, and with their invaluable assistance, the firemen were able to get the engine all the way to the hydrant. By Saturday dawn, the San Francisco Fire Department had managed to extinguish the last of the great fires in the southern part of the city.

While firefighters and their civilian helpers were battling the Mission District blaze, the fire that had rolled eastward from dynamited Van Ness Avenue toward Russian Hill and North Beach on Friday afternoon was consuming house after house. In one of the largest sea evacuations in history, 18 naval officers and sailors from the U.S.S. *Chicago* rescued an estimated 20,000 North Beach residents, transporting them across the bay to Tiburon in Marin County.

Although much of the two districts ultimately burned to the ground by this conflagration and a second one that had swept in earlier from the opposite direction, a handful of residents on the crest of Russian Hill did manage to save their homes. As the fires crept up Russian Hill, the homeowners stubbornly refused to be evacuated by the military. Instead they beat back the flames with brooms, rugs, and pails of any liquid they could find, including water from an old cistern, wine, and vinegar. Because of their courageous actions, after the fires had finally

Freeman Keeps the Order on the Waterfront

After U.S. Navy Lieutenant Frederick Freeman arrived in San Francisco on Wednesday, April 18, he quickly decided that he had two overwhelming responsibilities: first, to preserve the waterfront from flames and, second, to reestablish and maintain order in the city's easternmost fringes while the police force was occupied elsewhere. Freeman showed exceptional leadership skills in organizing and carrying out the second of these two self-imposed responsibilities, Midshipman John Pond later wrote of his commander:

Lieutenant Freeman had no instructions with regard to his position as far as preserving order was concerned, but he was not a man who would wait for instructions before taking action in an emergency. He was a born leader of men, a skipper whose men would go to Hell and back for him. . . .
   In the absence of uniformed police, Lieutenant Freeman assumed complete control of the waterfront district. His

burned themselves out in the district late Friday, a small grouping of structures still stood atop otherwise barren Russian Hill, rather "like tufts of hair atop a bald head," wrote Philip Fradkin in *The Great Earthquake and Firestorms of 1906*.

LIEUTENANT FREDERICK FREEMAN SAVES THE WATERFRONT

The long battle to save San Francisco's bay waterfront, the city's lifeline to the rest of the world, began shortly after the

orders were instantly obeyed and his authority was recognized without question by all, officials and civilians alike. Even his superiors refrained from interfering, and gave him a free hand, recognizing him as the man for the job.

On Friday, April 20, with a dangerous new fire rapidly approaching the precious wharves and warehouses of the north waterfront, however, Freeman found that even his commanding presence was not enough to keep the order. Later, he described the desperate measures he felt compelled to take that day to prevent panicky civilians from interfering with his and his men's firefighting duties:

Great trouble was experienced in controlling matters on East Street [a long, curving road that bordered the waterfront]. People hysterically endeavoring to escape the flames drove down East Street at frantic speed over the hose lines, bursting the overworking hose at frequent intervals. It was finally necessary to station sentries at all corners with orders to shoot down horses whose owners drove over hose faster than a walk.

earthquake hit on Wednesday morning and lasted until the early hours of Saturday, April 21. Throughout this period, the leader of the fight to preserve the waterfront was Navy Lieutenant Frederick Freeman, a man of remarkable organizational ability, dedication, and stamina.

Lieutenant Freeman and his men arrived at San Francisco on the destroyer U.S.S. *Preble* from the nearby Naval Training Station at Mare Island at about 10:00 Wednesday morning. Upon landing, Freeman went to work directing navy sailors and marines in pumping bay water from the *Leslie*, a fireboat, and the *Active*, a tug, at the many vulnerable wooden wharves and warehouses lining the waterfront along East Street. All through Wednesday and into the early hours of Thursday, Freeman and his squads labored to defend San Francisco's economically vital eastern fringes. Around 2:00 A.M. on Thursday, while the Fire Department was preoccupied with other blazes, Freeman and his men single-handedly prevented the city's other chief lifeline to the outside world from going up in flames—the Southern Pacific rail yards on Townsend Street in southeastern San Francisco.

With the fires along the waterfront under control—at least for the time being—on Thursday Freeman organized squads of sailors and marines to patrol the crime-ridden waterfront area, which the overextended police and army forces had largely ignored since the earthquake. Later in the day, he and his men turned their attention westward to one of the few unburned parts of the downtown, a small but heavily built-up area between Portsmouth Square and the Custom House. By laboriously running a hose from the bay for nearly a dozen city blocks, they were able to save one of San Francisco's most imposing and historic buildings, the Montgomery Block at the foot of Montgomery (later Columbus) Avenue. The following afternoon and evening, fire threatened the north waterfront. Although on the verge of collapse after being on duty for nearly three days straight, Freeman and his men fought courageously to defend the area's docks and warehouses, furiously spraying

After the earthquake's tremors subsided, the residents of Russian Hill sat outside their homes and watched as fire consumed their city *(above)*. Most Russian Hill residents eventually evacuated, though some stayed and managed to save their homes from the blaze.

seawater at the shorefront from the decks of the *Leslie* and *Active* even as hot embers rained down on them. "The hardest fight we had during the fire was at this point," Freeman later recalled: "A sulfur works was burning, the wind was blowing a gale, and showers of cinders, some three or four inches square, made this spot a purgatory. . . ."

THE WORST URBAN FIRE IN AMERICAN HISTORY

Finally, at around 6:00 A.M. Saturday, the fire on the north waterfront—the last of the significant blazes in the city—petered out. Because of the heroic actions of Freeman and his men, most of the piers had been saved.

By this time, San Francisco had been burning for approximately 72 hours. Later on Saturday, rain that would have been extremely welcome on Wednesday, Thursday, or Friday finally arrived. Despite the almost superhuman efforts made by some members of the military and by San Francisco firemen, many of whom worked with virtually no rest for three days and nights, the fires had taken a devastating toll on the city. In all, 28,818 buildings with an estimated property value of $400 million ($8.2 billion in today's dollars) were destroyed, and 225,000 people—more than half the city's residents—were left homeless. Gone were more than 500 city blocks—an area of 4.7 square miles. It was the worst urban fire in American history, more destructive even than the notorious Chicago Fire of 1871. Coping with the medical, economic, and social consequences of the San Francisco fire and earthquake of April 1906 would pose tremendous challenges both for the area's political and military leadership and its ordinary citizens.

6 Coping with the Catastrophe

No one knows exactly how many people died as a result of the earthquake and fires that devastated San Francisco between April 18 and April 21, 1906. Many bodies were never recovered, having been completely incinerated in the blazes' intense heat. Adding to the confusion, birth documents, marriage certificates, and scores of other public records were destroyed when the ruins of City Hall burned on the afternoon of April 18. Despite the difficulties involved in determining the number of fatalities from the disaster, within a few months of the quake and fire San Francisco officials reported a death toll of 498 out of a pre-earthquake population of just over 400,000. This tally struck many San Franciscans as surprisingly low, and some people even suspected that the municipal government, anxious to portray the city as a safe place to live and do business, deliberately underestimated the mortality rate.

Despite these widespread doubts, the official death toll for the great San Francisco temblor and fire of 1906 remained unchallenged for nearly a century. Finally, following an exhaustive examination of probate, hospital, cemetery, and orphanage

The towers of the St. Ignatius church burn as onlookers evacuate the area. After the first earthquake, residents who could leave gathered their belongings and headed towards the nearest ferry or train station. Later, as the city burned, the streets were clogged with buggies, pianos, horses, and baby carriages.

records; newspaper obituaries; and other contemporary sources, during the 1990s, San Francisco City archivist Gladys Hansen announced a new and dramatically higher death count for the catastrophe. According to Hansen, the quake and fire claimed at least 3,000 lives in San Francisco, a number that most scholars now accept as much closer to the true tally than the 498 fatalities reported by city officials back in 1906.

FLEEING

Yet, whether several thousand or several hundred died as a result of the earthquake and fire of April 1906, the fact remains that the vast majority of San Francisco's population managed to survive the disaster. More than 200,000 survivors fled the ravaged city between Wednesday, April 18, and Saturday, April 21, when the fires finally petered out. Large numbers of evacuees flocked to the relatively undamaged Ferry Building at the foot of Market Street. From there, most caught a ferry to Oakland, on the eastern side of San Francisco Bay. Many others departed the city by rail; from 6:00 A.M. Wednesday until Sunday evening, April 22, the Southern Pacific railroad waived all fares for fleeing San Franciscans. The rush of panicky citizens for the ferry and railway stations began within minutes of the earthquake, picking up steam as a series of aftershocks rattled the city and caused loose brickwork to rain down on the streets and sidewalks. (Aftershocks are milder shudders that follow the main shock of the earthquake.) The exodus from San Francisco continued unabated for the next 72 hours.

To get themselves and their belongings to the stations as quickly as possible, wealthy San Franciscans often hired horse-drawn wagons or automobiles at exorbitant prices. Jack London reported overhearing a man offer a driver $1,000 for the use of his team of horses to transport several large trunks to the docks. The military was supposed to appropriate all motorized and horse-drawn vehicles in the city to transport the injured, doctors, and city officials and haul explosives or other firefighting equipment. Nonetheless, wrote Dan Kurzman, "Many unauthorized drivers continued to operate them—until stopped by soldiers, some of whom would become 'reasonable' on hearing the jingle of gold coins."

Most of those who fled San Francisco between April 18 and April 21, however, were forced to make their way to the ferries or railway depot on foot. Consequently, they were only able to bring with them whatever they could carry or push or drag along the streets. Marion Leale, a ferry captain's daughter who lived near the waterfront, watched as a steady stream of refugees hurried past her house toward the docks bearing an amazingly wide assortment of personal possessions, from the practical to the frivolous. "Thousands swept past," Leale recalled, "wheeling baby carriages, sewing machines, carpet sweepers and other ridiculous as well as pathetic treasures." A number of people carried pet birds in cages, and at one point, Leale heard a parrot squawking, "'My God this is awful! My God this is terrible!'" over and

Jack London on San Francisco's Refugees

On Wednesday night, April 18, Jack London wandered through the heart of San Francisco, observing the thousands of fire and earthquake refugees who filled the streets. The following excerpts are from his poignant account of the disaster for *Collier's* magazine, published in May 1906:

Before the flames, throughout the night, fled tens of thousands of homeless ones. Some were wrapped in blankets. Others carried bundles of bedding and dear household treasures. Sometimes a whole family was harnessed to a carriage or delivery wagon that was weighted down with their possessions. Baby buggies, toy wagons, and go-carts were used as trucks, while every other person was dragging a trunk. . . .

All night these tens of thousands fled before the flames. Many of them, the poor people from the labor ghetto, had fled all day as well. They had left their homes burdened with over again. "Those who saw it," she concluded, "will never forget this evacuation."

STAYING BEHIND

Not all of the survivors fled town in the immediate aftermath of the earthquake: As many as half of the city's inhabitants stayed in the San Francisco area in the wake of the disaster. A majority of those who remained vacated their homes during the hours and days following the temblor, however. In many

possessions. Now and again they lightened up, flinging out upon the street clothing and treasures they had dragged for miles.

They held on longest to their trunks, and over these trunks many a strong man broke his heart that night. The hills of San Francisco are steep, and up these hills, mile after mile, were the trunks dragged. Everywhere were trunks with across them lying their exhausted owners, men and women. Before the march of the flames were flung picket lines of soldiers. And a block at a time, as the flames advanced, these pickets retreated. One of their tasks was to keep the trunk-pullers moving. The exhausted creatures, stirred on by the menace of bayonets, would arise and struggle up the steep pavements, pausing from weakness every five or ten feet.

Often, after surmounting a heart-breaking hill, they would find another wall of flame advancing upon them at right angles and be compelled to change anew the line of their retreat. In the end, completely played out, after toiling for a dozen hours like giants, thousands of them were compelled to abandon their trunks. . . .

cases, they had no choice: Their houses or apartment buildings had been severely damaged by the earthquake or stood in the path of approaching fires. Yet, even many San Franciscans whose dwellings had survived the shaking intact and were situated well away from the fires chose to leave their homes during the uncertain days following the quake. Fearful of another temblor, they felt safer sleeping outside in parks, on military land, or in vacant lots than under their own roofs.

Following the quake, tens of thousands of San Franciscans sought shelter on the western side of the city in spacious Golden Gate Park or at the vast U.S. Army base, the Presidio. Typically, they lugged as many personal belongings with them as they could manage, either in big trunks or piled high on anything with wheels, from baby buggies to trash wagons. Observers described the western migrants as somber-faced and silent. Often the only sound that could be heard as they passed by was the scraping of dozens of heavy trunks being dragged over the pavement. "The sickening sound of grating on the concrete entered so deep into my brain that I think it will never leave it," one eyewitness who lived along a main route to the Presidio later remarked.

THE ARMY AND THE RED CROSS TO THE RESCUE

Many of the people who headed for the Presidio during the disaster sought not only refuge "under the protecting arms of Uncle Sam," as one army major put it, but also medical treatment at the post's two hospitals. By noon Wednesday, the Presidio was receiving wagon- and carloads of injured men, women, and children from many quake- and fire-ravaged neighborhoods. Hundreds of them were transported to the base from the Mechanics' Pavilion. A large athletic arena and convention center one block from City Hall, Mechanics' Pavilion was hastily transformed into a hospital ward when the Central Emergency Hospital located in the basement of the municipal building was severely damaged during the first seconds of shaking. About 11:00 A.M., sparks from nearby fires ignited the roof of the Mechanics' Pavilion, necessitating a transfer of the makeshift hospital's approximately 300 patients to the Presidio. Over the next month, hundreds more civilian patients received medical assistance at the base. During the same period, thousands more San Franciscans were given free medical attention at an army field hospital that was hastily erected in Golden Gate Park soon after the quake.

Aside from providing much-needed medical assistance to the city's residents, the army also furnished food, clean drinking water, clothing, and blankets to tens of thousands of San Franciscans for weeks following the disaster. Overwhelmed by the enormity of the task of caring for the huge numbers of destitute and displaced San Franciscans, Mayor Schmitz and the Committee of Fifty (reorganized as the Committee of Forty by the end of April) relied heavily on the army to help distribute both military and civil supplies. And there certainly was no shortage of supplies to dispense: As early as Thursday, donations of food and other necessities as well as cash had begun flooding into San Francisco from towns and cities, charitable and religious organizations, businesses and individuals, all over California and the United States. Working closely with the Red Cross, the army set up food and clothing depots throughout the devastated sections of San Francisco to ensure that the donations made it to those who needed them most.

The American Red Cross, although still a relatively young and untried organization at the time, would play a central part in San Francisco's relief efforts. The leading force behind the Red Cross's pivotal role in managing the disaster was President Theodore Roosevelt. He entrusted the nonprofit organization with distributing funds from the federal government in Washington, D.C., as well as large contributions from state and municipal governments and individual donors such as millionaires Andrew Carnegie and John D. Rockefeller. Well aware of Schmitz's reputation for dishonesty, Roosevelt wanted the aid, which eventually totaled $9 million, including $2.5 million in federal relief funds, to go directly to the Red Cross rather than San Francisco's political leadership. By late April, however, Roosevelt had agreed

While half of San Francisco's population evacuated the city, the other half stayed behind. Because most buildings were either in danger of collapsing or being consumed by fire, many remaining residents slept on the army base or in open-air areas like Golden Gate Park. Left without the means to feed their own families, people cooked food donated by the Army on makeshift fires or communal stoves that were constructed for the camps.

to let political reformer and onetime San Francisco mayor, James Phelan, chairman of the Committee of Forty's finance subcommittee, to receive and distribute disaster relief funds along with the American Red Cross's chief representative in San Francisco, Dr. Edward Devine.

ORGANIZING REFUGEE CAMPS AND ENFORCING SANITATION MEASURES

Some 250,000 San Franciscans—more than half the city's population—were left homeless by the earthquake and fires. Many of them sought temporary lodging in the scores of small and large refugee camps that sprang up all over the city from Wednesday onward.

By far the biggest, cleanest, and most efficiently run of the various refugee camps were organized by the army. In all, the army constructed and oversaw 21 relief camps in the Presidio, Fort Mason, Golden Gate Park, and other city parks and squares. Residents were housed in neatly arranged tents or simple wooden barracks and took their meals in military-style mess halls. Bathing, toilet, and laundry facilities were communal. Although life in the camps was far from luxurious, many refugees were determined to make the best of the situation, organizing playgroups for their children and forging new friendships in the camps' chief social centers, the mess halls.

Maintaining high sanitation standards was a top priority in the army-run refugee camps. To ensure proper sanitation practices and keep disease outbreaks to a minimum, an army medical officer closely supervised each camp. Any residents refusing to comply with camp sanitation regulations were promptly evicted. Because of widespread fears that the ruined city was the perfect breeding ground for contagious disease, the army also agreed to work with the San Francisco Board of Health to enforce strict sanitation rules regarding garbage disposal, latrines, and drinking water throughout San Francisco. Largely as a result of the army's efforts, which included daily inspections of every refugee camp in the city, although typhoid fever and smallpox claimed some victims, San Francisco escaped any major outbreaks of infectious disease during the months following the disaster.

CONCERNS REGARDING THE MILITARY'S ROLE

Despite the military's invaluable assistance in providing medical care and housing for disaster victims and enforcing sanitation regulations in the city, some of their actions during the days and weeks following the temblor were highly controversial. San Franciscans were particularly disturbed by the military's conscription (drafting) of civilians to clear rubble and their on-the-spot executions of suspected looters.

Martial law is the temporary rule of an area by military authorities during an emergency when the usual civil authorities are judged unable to function effectively. Not surprisingly, most San Franciscans assumed that martial law had gone into effect in their hometown on Wednesday morning, April 18, when approximately 1,000 rifle-toting, U.S. Army troops descended on the city with orders to shoot suspected criminals on sight. This perception was only reinforced when several hundred members of other military groups, including the Marines, Navy, and California National Guard, soon joined army troops in patrolling San Francisco's streets. Yet despite appearances, martial law was never officially proclaimed in San Francisco after the earthquake. Only the president of the United States may declare martial law on the federal level and governors on the state level, and neither President Roosevelt nor Governor Pardee decided to take that step in April 1906.

Believing that their city was under martial law—and intimidated by the soldiers' rifles—most San Franciscans submitted to the troops' orders, even those they considered as misguided or unjust. For example, many people resented

Martial law was never declared in San Francisco, but residents felt threatened and resentful of the soldiers who they believed abused their power. Signs such as the one above were posted all over the city and warned people to "obey orders or get shot." Many citizens were shot on sight, without any questions or investigation of their actions.

being forced at gunpoint to evacuate relatively fire-resistant brick office buildings, shops, or homes, structures that they firmly believed they and their employees or neighbors could have saved from the flames, if given the chance. Other San Franciscans such as businessman John Jorgensen complained of being conscripted into work gangs by rifle-brandishing soldiers. Jorgensen had been visiting Oakland when the earthquake struck, and on Saturday, April 21, Governor Pardee gave him special permission to return to his ravaged hometown to attend to pressing business matters. However, no sooner had he walked out of the ferry station on Market Street, Jorgensen recalled, than "I was halted by an officer with a big revolver and pressed into service, viz, [namely] heaving brick. . . . The soldiers were always in the way with their bayonets ready to shoot the first man who refused to obey."

The shooting of suspected looters by soldiers and specially deputized civilians also deeply disturbed many San Franciscans, including photojournalist Moshe Cohen, who saw three uniformed men kill another man as he was running out of a store with an armload of merchandise. "It all made me sick," Cohen wrote:

> The stuff the man had taken would have been burned anyhow. The fire was only a block away. . . . And there's always the question that kept dogging me. How did they know that he wasn't entitled to the stuff? He could have worked in the place, or maybe even been one of the owners. Maybe he ran because he was scared, . . . as he was entitled to be, with three guns pointing at him. But none of those soldiers even bothered to find out.

The army later claimed that only two men were shot in San Francisco for looting between April 18 and July 1, 1906, when the last troops finally departed the city, but newspaper and eyewitness accounts contradict that claim. Although the exact number of San Franciscans killed by military forces and civilian deputies is unknown, many historians believe that at least 50 people were shot, most of them during the first 72 hours following the earthquake. "The division of authority between army and municipality brought some terrible results," wrote Marion Osgood Hooker, a San Francisco physician: "The military was called in to take partial command; the citizens did not know whom they were to obey, and certainly the military subordinates and guards were not made to understand the limits of their authority. The consequences were tragic. Preserve us from our preservers was the cry of many of us."

Not everyone shared Dr. Hooker's concerns regarding the sweeping authority assumed by the military in San Francisco after the earthquake, however. Writer Mary Austin, for instance, found the military's presence in the city profoundly reassuring during the chaotic days after the earthquake hit. Moreover, she was convinced that many other San Franciscans shared her conviction that desperate times called for desperate measures: "The will of the people was toward authority, and everywhere the tread of soldiery brought a relieved sense of things orderly and secure. It was not as if the city had waited for martial law to be declared, but as if it precipitated itself into that state by instinct as its best refuge."

7 Rebuilding

Except for the Western Addition, the waterfront, and the southern sections of the Mission District, the fires caused by the great earthquake of April 18, 1906, had left the once-thriving city of San Francisco a blackened wasteland. "The fire had done its work thoroughly, leaving nothing half burned," wrote newspaper editor Charles Sedgwick. "Streets were no longer defined, no longer recognizable, and were still as a desert. The whole scene resembled more some ancient ruins in Egypt or Greece from which the dust of ages had recently been removed, than a modern American metropolis."

CLEARING THE RUBBLE

The mammoth task of rebuilding the ruined city began almost immediately after the last fires were extinguished on the morning of Saturday, April 21, 1906. The earthquake and fire had disabled San Francisco's water, electric, and gas systems and demolished its public transportation system and most of its libraries, schools, hotels, retail stores, wholesale houses, banks, and private residences. Despite the scope of the destruction, however, the city's political and business leaders were determined to get San Francisco on its feet again as soon as possible. By Sunday, April 22, several hundred plumbers were already repairing the broken water pipes, and by the end of the month, new electric streetcars were running in the downtown district.

For the first two weeks after the earthquake and fire, the military conscripted able-bodied civilians to remove the tons of rubble clogging San Francisco's streets. After that, the city paid thousands of professional laborers to complete the arduous undertaking. Two of the Bay Area's leading transportation companies took a major role in organizing the cleanup, as laborer H.C. Graves later described: "The United Railroads in cooperation with the SP [Southern Pacific Railroad] undertook the huge task of clearing the business section of downtown San

The first Chinese in San Francisco arrived in 1848. Nearly six decades later, on the eve of the great earthquake of 1906, approximately 25,000 Chinese people lived in San Francisco's Chinatown. When the earthquake and fire destroyed all the buildings and structures of the neighborhood *(above)*, the Chinese community was determined to rebuild but was faced with governmental opposition.

Francisco of the debris. The millions of bricks that were good were stripped of old mortar, and piled up on all the streets. The United Railroads built a big bunker at First and Mission . . . and dump trucks drawn by horses hauled the debris up to the bunkers." According to one account, more than 10,000 draft horses were worked to death in San Francisco during the year and a half following the earthquake and fire. "Their lives are a sacrifice to an exigency [pressing need] of the times," wrote a contemporary journalist.

Most of the estimated 11 million cubic yards of rubble generated by the disaster were dumped into a marsh near the north waterfront. This resulted in the creation of many acres of new "made land," on which scores of buildings were eventually constructed, despite the violent and highly destructive shaking that had occurred on the city's made ground during the 1906 earthquake. The focus of San Francisco's political and business leaders was on reconstructing the city as quickly as possible, and in their haste to rebuild, practical safety concerns were ignored more often than not. City leaders were also in too much of a hurry to rebuild to seriously contemplate any significant changes in San Francisco's layout. Two years before the earthquake, a group of prominent San Franciscans had hired the respected urban planner Daniel H. Burnham to develop a beautification scheme for their city, whose streets formed a simple—and in the view of some, unattractive—grid pattern. Now that most of the city had been leveled, it seemed like the perfect time to implement Burnham's graceful design, which included grand new boulevards and an extension of Golden Gate Park eastward toward the downtown. Concerned that adopting the architect's ambitious plan would only slow down the rebuilding process, however, city leaders rejected virtually all of Burnham's recommendations and decided to reconstruct the city on its original street grid. The city fathers did want to make one major change in the old layout of the city and its neighborhoods, however: They wanted to get rid of Chinatown.

THE FIGHT OVER CHINATOWN

The 16 crowded city blocks that made up Chinatown had been virtually razed by the earthquake and fire, leaving thousands of residents homeless. Many Chinese fled the city for Oakland, where they were shunted to a segregated relief camp on the outskirts of town. Others settled in a segregated refugee camp at the Presidio or set up their own small camps on the fringes of the city. To their dismay, the refugees soon heard that a committee had been organized by the mayor to permanently relocate all of San Francisco's ethnic Chinese residents to a new "Oriental City" on Hunter's Point, six miles away from their old neighborhood. Hunter's Point was a barren peninsula on the city's southeastern outskirts. Because of Chinatown's central location, the municipal government asserted, the area had excellent potential for commercial development. As far as the committee members were concerned, a prime piece of real estate was no place for a Chinese ghetto.

The plan to push the Chinese out of their longtime home to a more remote part of the city had clear racist overtones, and the empress dowager of China was deeply offended by the scheme. Through her emissaries in the United States, the empress let President Roosevelt know in no uncertain terms that her people in San Francisco had a right to live wherever they chose. Not wanting to damage diplomatic relations—and a lucrative economic trade—with China, Roosevelt pressured San Francisco's political leaders into abandoning the idea.

Ironically, the earthquake and fires that leveled Chinatown in April 1906 had a silver lining for its residents. All of the birth certificates stored in City Hall had burned on the day of the earthquake. According to the racist laws of the era, only Chinese born in the United States could become U.S. citizens.

After the disaster, hundreds of native Chinese in San Francisco were able to become U.S. citizens by claiming that the birth certificates that supposedly proved their American birthplaces had burned in the fire. A second unexpected boon for Chinese San Franciscans was Chinatown's unprecedented ability to attract tourist dollars after its rebuilding. The exotic appearance of many of the neighborhood's reconstructed buildings was at the heart of its new appeal. Local Chinese merchants were behind the district's fresh look, which featured brightly colored tiled roofs, curved eaves, and other Chinese motifs that were not necessarily authentic but which shop and restaurant

Witnessing the Best and Worst of Human Nature After the Earthquake

Guion Dewey, a businessman from Virginia, was staying at the Palace Hotel when the earthquake struck on Wednesday, April 18, 1906. During the shaking, he suffered a painful broken jaw. Wandering onto the streets of downtown San Francisco minutes after the quake in search of medical assistance, the Virginian experienced the best and worst of human behavior, as he later reported in a letter to his mother:

I saw innocent men shot down by the irresponsible militia. I walked four miles to have my jaw set. A stranger tried to make me accept a $10 gold piece. I was threatened with death for trying to help a small girl drag a trunk from a burning house, where her father and mother had been killed. A strange man gave me raw eggs and milk . . . (the owners correctly surmised would please the tourists. "It was a[n] ingenious move, selling a fake China to those white folks who didn't know any better; and the Chinese community since survived with a degree of prosperity on its own despite intense racial prejudice and discrimination," wrote Professor Marlon Hom of San Francisco State University.

A CONSTRUCTION BOOM AND "EARTHQUAKE COTTAGES"

By the autumn of 1906, much of the rubble had been cleared from San Francisco's streets, and tens of thousands of carpenters,

first food I had had for twenty-two hours). I saw a soldier shoot a horse because its driver allowed it to drink at a fire hose which had burst. I had a Catholic priest kneel by me in the park as I lay on a bed of alfalfa hay, covered with a piece of carpet, and pray to the Holy Father for relief for my pain. . . . I saw a poor woman, barefoot, told to "Go to Hell and be glad for it" for asking for a glass of milk at a dairyman's wagon; she had in her arms a baby with its legs broken. I gave her a dollar and walked with her to the hospital. . . .

I was pressed into service by an officer, who made me help to strike tents in front of the St. Francis Hotel, when the order was issued to dynamite all buildings in the vicinity to save the hotel. I like him, and hope to meet him again. When he saw I was hurt, which I had not told him, not yet having been bandaged, he took me to his own tent and gave me water and brandy and a clean handkerchief.

bricklayers, plumbers, and other skilled and unskilled laborers from all over the United States were hard at work building
schools, libraries, stores, restaurants, theaters, office buildings,
hospitals, parks, and houses. In the downtown business district,
there was a new emphasis on constructing modern, steel-framed
buildings not only because they were relatively fire-resistant but
also because metal- and particularly steel-girded structures had
held up well during the quake. In 1907, a report by the American
Society of Civil Engineers explained the superiority of steel-
framed buildings in earthquakes. Steel's natural elasticity, the
report noted, allowed it to move with the temblor's vibrations
rather than snapping under the stress.

Yet, despite the greater number of steel-girded buildings
being constructed in the downtown district, scores of hastily
and poorly made wood-frame houses once again cropped up
in the city's working-class neighborhoods, even in those that
rested on made land, where the last temblor had taken such
a terrible toll. In 1907, the respected San Francisco architect
Willis Polk cautioned that "many buildings are now being
constructed in a manner that will court certain destruction in
case of another earthquake." No one seemed much concerned
about Polk's warning, however; the focus was on rebuilding the
ruined city as quickly and as inexpensively as possible "with
scant regard for future cataclysms," noted Phillip Fradkin.

As houses and apartment buildings began to spring up
throughout the city's devastated neighborhoods, many San
Franciscans who had fled to Oakland and elsewhere returned,
and by July 1906, city officials reported 375,000 registered
residents. With assistance from the army, municipal authorities designed and built some of the new housing for the
refugees. In the autumn of 1906, city leaders, eager to clear
out as many of the relief camps as possible, funded the construction of more than 5,000 wooden "earthquake cottages"
for low-income families in parks and other public land. The
government charged two dollars a month in rent for the small

one- to three-room cottages, money that could be used toward their purchase as long as the buyer agreed to have the house moved onto a private lot. By mid-1907, all of the modest government-sponsored homes had been sold and hauled off public lands, and a year later, San Francisco's last refugee camps were finally shut down.

FUNDING THE REBUILDING

The expensive task of rebuilding San Francisco was largely funded by two sources: bank loans and insurance payouts. San Francisco had long been the financial center of the American West; by the early 1900s, its banks handled more money than all other banks west of the Mississippi combined. Moreover, much of the federal government's gold and silver reserves were stored in the U.S. Mint, which mint employees had courageously saved from the flames on the day of the earthquake.

The majority of San Francisco's banks were unable to access their funds for some time after the disaster, however. Most kept their money and financial securities in metal vaults in their downtown offices. The vaults survived the flames, but because of the extremely high temperatures generated by the fires, bank officials were afraid to open them right away. Immediately after the Great Chicago Fire of 1871, money and bank records had spontaneously combusted when bank employees unlocked their vaults and let in a rush of oxygen before the scorching air inside had had a chance to cool down. Taking their cue from the Chicago debacle, San Francisco bankers decided to wait for two full weeks before opening their vaults.

One quick-thinking San Francisco banker did manage to retrieve all of his institution's funds on the day of the earthquake. The Bank of Italy, a small bank on Columbus Avenue founded only two years earlier by Italian-American businessman Amadeo Giannini, provided loans to recent immigrants and working people, two groups who were typically turned away by loan officers at the city's major banks. On April 18, as fire spread through the city, Giannini borrowed horses and a produce wagon and raced to his bank, determined to empty its vaults before the flames closed in. After stuffing bank records and $80,000 in gold and silver in the back of the wagon under crates of oranges, he slipped out of the city to his home in San Mateo. A few days later, the Bank of Italy became the first San Francisco bank to reopen when Giannini set up a makeshift office on the Washington Street wharf with two barrels topped by a plank for his desk. Soon he was providing modest loans to scores of small businessmen and homeowners anxious to rebuild their lives. Renamed the Bank of America in 1930, today Giannini's little San Francisco enterprise is the biggest commercial bank in the United States and the third largest in the world. Within a few weeks of the Bank of Italy's reopening, most of San Francisco's banks had also opened for business and begun handing out millions of dollars in loans that were to prove vital to the reconstruction of city.

Along with bank loans, insurance payouts were also a critical source of funds for the rebuilding of San Francisco. Most business owners and homeowners had fire insurance, but none had earthquake insurance, which did not become generally available in the United States until the mid-1920s. After the disaster, dozens of American and foreign insurance companies sent adjusters to meticulously examine each and every claim on the basis of fire as opposed to earthquake damage, significantly slowing down the awarding of settlements. All in all, nearly 100,000 claims were processed by more than 200 different insurance companies. The firms had a decidedly mixed record. Only six companies paid their policyholders in full; many others paid significantly less than the claims, sometimes no more than 5 to 10 percent of a policy's value. Nonetheless, in the end, San Franciscans received some $250 million in payouts—about $5 billion in current dollars—to reconstruct their damaged homes, businesses, and other property.

"WE DO NOT BELIEVE IN ADVERTISING THE EARTHQUAKE"

Almost immediately after the disaster, as San Francisco began to rebuild, its political and business leaders launched a concerted public relations campaign designed to minimize the earthquake's role in wrecking the city. Newspaper and magazine reporters were encouraged to characterize the calamity as "the great fire" rather than "the great earthquake," and city officials attributed most deaths and virtually all of the

As refugees returned to San Francisco, local authorities were faced with a housing shortage. "Earthquake cottages" were built for those who needed temporary housing but could also be purchased as permanent housing by those who were less fortunate. *Above*, the last two cottages remaining in the Presidio are preserved and were photographed on the 100th anniversary of the earthquake and fire.

structural damage in San Francisco to the fires as opposed to the temblor. Needless to say, the inconvenient fact that the fires were a direct result of the violent shaking that ruptured gas mains, overturned stoves and lamps, and brought down electrical wires was ignored.

In de-emphasizing the severity and destructiveness of the earthquake and stressing the fires instead, San Francisco's leaders hoped to reduce any negative economic impact that the disaster might have on the city. They worried that potential investors, residents, and businesses would be scared off if San Francisco developed a reputation as an earthquake-prone area. Earthquakes were widely viewed as an unpredictable and uncontrollable act of God. Fires, on the other hand, a hazard to which all U.S. cities were susceptible, were viewed as potentially preventable and controllable, for example, by the adoption of stringent fire safety measures or the purchase of more and better firefighting equipment.

According to a scientist on the State Earthquake Investigation Commission appointed by Governor Pardee to study the San Francisco quake in 1906, geologists were "advised and even urged over and over again" (by many political and business leaders alike) to keep geological data on the temblor to themselves. One of the chief players in the campaign to divert attention away from the earthquake was the Southern Pacific Company, which not only owned or rented out all of the major railroad lines into the city but also possessed extensive real estate in San Francisco. Within weeks of the disaster, the company's general passenger agent, James Horsburgh, wrote to every Chamber of Commerce in the state of California: "The real calamity in San Francisco was undoubtedly the fire. . . . We do not believe in advertising the earthquake."

Most historians of the San Francisco tragedy agree that the public relations campaign to erase the temblor from the story of the city's devastation and focus solely on the conflagration was effective. Indeed, so effective was the campaign, many scholars have noted, that for decades afterward San Franciscans typically referred to the disaster as the great fire of 1906 rather than as the great earthquake and fire of 1906.

8 Into the Future

The rebuilding of San Francisco after the earthquake and fire of April 1906 progressed more quickly than anyone could have imagined. By 1909, most of the ruined parts of the city had been reconstructed. Remarkably, 20,000 new buildings had been erected in the space of just three years to replace the 28,800 leveled during the disaster. In 1915, San Francisco proudly showed off its rapid recovery to the rest of the world. That year, the city hosted a gigantic world's fair, the Panama-Pacific International Exposition, to celebrate the opening of the Panama Canal and the 400th anniversary of Vasco Núñez de Balboa's discovery of the Pacific Ocean. The event, which lasted for nine months, attracted millions of visitors. By this time, the city boasted a modern new Hall of Justice and county hospital and, most impressive of all, a magnificent new Civic Center. Featuring two spacious plazas and a large public library, among other buildings, the Civic Center was constructed around an elegant new City Hall crowned by a dome that was higher than the U.S. Capitol in Washington and patterned after the cupola of St. Peter's Basilica in Rome.

When the splendid new City Hall was officially dedicated in late 1915 shortly after the end of the Panama-Pacific Exposition, "Handsome Gene" Schmitz did not officiate at the ceremony as San Francisco's chief executive. That honor went to James Rolph, the city's mayor since 1910. For a brief time, the catastrophe of April 1906 had diverted attention from the graft investigation of Schmitz and his crony, Abe Ruef, which had been launched on the eve of the earthquake and fire. But Schmitz and Ruef's chief critics, editor Fremont Older, millionaire Rudolph Spreckels, and ex-mayor James Phelan, had no intention of abandoning their crusade to clean up San Francisco's government. By late 1906, they had convinced President Roosevelt to send a special prosecutor from Washington to indict the mayor and his right-hand man on suspicion of corruption. In June 1907, Schmitz and Ruef were found guilty of extortion and sentenced to prison. Schmitz's conviction was overturned on appeal just a year later, but Ruef was not as fortunate. He spent almost five years in San Quentin State Prison before being granted parole.

PREPARING FOR ANOTHER DISASTER IN THE WAKE OF THE APRIL 1906 CALAMITY

San Francisco's rapid reconstruction was a source of enormous pride for its residents. Their city, San Franciscans felt, had more than lived up to its official seal, which features the legendary phoenix bird. According to ancient myth, when it becomes old and feeble the phoenix consumes itself in flame. Soon after, the colorfully plumed bird rises miraculously from its own ashes, young and strong once more. Today, many people assume that the phoenix was adopted as San Francisco's official emblem after the 1906 earthquake and fire. In truth, it was selected to adorn San Francisco's seal in 1859, decades before the disaster, in honor of the city's successful rebuilding after six devastating fires during the Gold Rush era of the late 1840s and early 1850s.

San Francisco's speedy recovery after being nearly wiped out in 1906 was certainly impressive. Yet the haste with which San Francisco was reconstructed had a big drawback: The city's dash to rebuild meant that future safety considerations were all too often sacrificed to expediency, including rebuilding on landfill despite the extremely poor performance of made ground on April 18. In the realm of fire prevention, San Francisco's building codes remained virtually unchanged after the disaster, and the few new safety measures that were adopted were not uniformly enforced. Much of the city's downtown district was supposed to be a fire-limits zone, where only buildings fabricated from fire-resistant materials could be

The Plague Strikes San Francisco

A year after the disaster of April 1906, San Francisco suffered an outbreak of one of the most dreaded diseases in human history: the bubonic plague. A frequently fatal bacterial illness, bubonic plague is transmitted to humans by fleas that have ingested blood from an infected rodent, usually a rat. High fever; weakness; and swollen, painful lymph nodes (called buboes) are the most common symptoms of the disease.

Bubonic plague had briefly terrorized San Francisco several years earlier in 1900, most likely arriving there on a Chinese merchant ship. This first outbreak, which infected about 100 people, was almost entirely confined to the impoverished Chinatown district. City officials, anxious to protect San Francisco's reputation as a safe place to live and do business, downplayed the outbreak in public. At the same time, however, they launched a campaign to clean up Chinatown's constructed. Yet, succumbing to pressure by powerful business interests anxious to rebuild as quickly and inexpensively as possible, city officials often overlooked this important safety requirement. Moreover, in many residential neighborhoods, wooden "row houses"—side-by-side houses joined by common walls—were built without fireproof dividers between them to help prevent the spread of fire.

Aside from the installation of a new fire alarm system housed in earthquake-resistant quarters, the one significant improvement in San Francisco's fire prevention standards after the 1906 conflagration was in the area of water supply. The 74-mile-long water-main system was redesigned to make

rat-infested streets and tenements, and by 1904, the disease had disappeared from the city.

In May 1907, plague flared up once more in San Francisco, which, despite the stringent sanitation regulations enforced by the army and city health officials, had seen an inevitable spike in its rat and flea populations in the wake of the earthquake and fire. Over the course of the following year, 160 San Franciscans were infected with the plague, and 77 died. This time around, however, government leaders made no effort to conceal the outbreak, which affected fire- and earthquake-devastated neighborhoods throughout the city. Far from downplaying the crisis, local and state officials enlisted the public's help in trapping San Francisco's swelling rat population, even offering bounties for the rodents. In all, more than a million rats were killed as part of the government-sponsored program. By the end of 1908, San Francisco's second and last plague crisis had passed.

As the fires died down and the tremors subsided, local authorities pushed to rebuild the city as quickly as possible but did little to reform or enforce building and fire codes that would minimize the damage of natural disasters. Despite having seen the benefits of using steel in construction *(above)*, business owners quickly erected new buildings with flimsy materials, and wooden structures, once again, popped up all over the city.

it easier to shut off water to earthquake-damaged parts of the city, thus preventing precious water from being lost into the ground through fractured pipes. Aging, underground cisterns were refurbished, and nearly 100 new ones capable of holding an average of 75,000 gallons of water were placed beneath street intersections. The city purchased two fireboats and installed two auxiliary pumping stations for drawing saltwater from the bay. Most importantly, the city oversaw the creation of a state-of-the-art, high-pressure freshwater supply system. The new freshwater system featured two mammoth distributing basins, containing 500,000 and 750,000 gallons each, which were supplied by an even bigger storage reservoir near the summit of San Francisco's loftiest hill, the Twin Peaks. The reason for the reservoir's high elevation was to take advantage of the pull of gravity to create greater water pressure for extinguishing fires quickly.

THE LOMA PRIETA EARTHQUAKE

Ever since the San Francisco earthquake of April 18, 1906, scientists have been warning that it is just a matter of time before another major temblor strikes the Bay Area. During the decades following the 1906 temblor, several moderate earthquakes measuring just over 5.0 on the Richter scale rattled the nerves of San Franciscans but caused only minor damage. Then, at 5:04 P.M., October 17, 1989, the first strong earthquake in the Bay Area in more than 83 years hit. The Loma Prieta earthquake, as the temblor came to be known, measured 6.9 on the moment magnitude scale and had an epicenter within the San Andreas Fault Zone, about 60 miles southeast of San Francisco in the Santa Cruz Mountains near Loma Prieta Mountain.

The city of Santa Cruz, just nine miles away from the quake's epicenter, was hardest hit. However, the costliest property damage from the temblor occurred in San Francisco and nearby Oakland. Most spectacularly, a section of the San Francisco–Oakland Bay Bridge split apart, killing one, and the

Cypress Street Viaduct on Oakland's double-decker freeway, Interstate 880, collapsed, crushing 41 motorists. In all, more than 60 people died and nearly 4,000 were injured as a result of the quake.

Within the city of San Francisco, ground shaking and damage were most severe in the made ground on the fringes of the bay, particularly in the upscale residential neighborhood known as the Marina District. Throughout the 24-square-block area, 35 buildings were completely destroyed and more than a hundred others damaged. The numerous fires that erupted when gas mains fractured in the liquefied ground added to the destruction in the Marina District. Since underground water lines were also severed, seawater had to be pumped out of the bay to douse the fires. Before the 1906 earthquake, most of the present-day Marina District had been underwater, but after the temblor, tons of debris from collapsed and burnt-out buildings was dumped there. In 1915, this soggy addition to northern San Francisco served as the site of the Panama-Pacific International Exposition. When the fair was over, nearly all the exposition halls and other structures especially constructed for the event were hastily demolished and used to further fill in what would soon become the new Marina District's unstable foundation.

ON SHAKY GROUND

Although total property damage from the Loma Prieta earthquake of 1989 was estimated at $6 billion—with about $3 billion of that amount in San Francisco itself—the magnitude 6.9 earthquake was actually significantly weaker than the 1906 temblor. While the 1989 earthquake falls under the "large earthquake" classification on the moment magnitude scale, the 1906 quake's estimated magnitude of 7.7–7.9 puts it at the high end of the scale's "major earthquake" designation. The destructive shaking also lasted for a significantly shorter time in 1989 than in 1906: just 15 seconds as opposed to 60–65 seconds. Furthermore, in sharp contrast to the earlier temblor, the epicenter of the Loma Prieta earthquake was more than 50 miles away from the city of San Francisco, instead of practically right underneath it.

Seismologists can say with certainty that another earthquake greater than the 1989 temblor—one on a par with the quake of 1906—will rock San Francisco again. Despite the advances that have been made in earthquake science since the 1906 earthquake, however, scientists still have no way

Not all of San Francisco had to be rebuilt, and parts of the city still contain houses dating to the nineteenth century. In the last few decades, business investments and tourism have turned the city into a thriving metropolis, one where new skyscrapers exist beside structures that have survived earthquakes and fires.

to predict the location, timing, and magnitude of future earthquakes with any degree of accuracy. Even so, scientists agree that the odds of another seismic disaster occurring in the Bay Area are overwhelming: The region is crisscrossed by no fewer than seven faults, including the San Andreas. In 2005, scientists at the University of California at Davis, using data from a state-of-the-art computer simulation program, set the probability of a major earthquake of magnitude 7.0 or higher striking the San Francisco area within the following two decades at 25 percent. That probability rises to just over 50 percent in the next half century, and to 75 percent in the next 80 years.

Over the past several decades, and particularly since the mid-1970s, when stringent new building codes were passed in the city, San Francisco has taken a number of important steps to minimize earthquake damage and fatalities from the next "Big One," whenever it may strike. Yet, while in recent years billions of dollars have been spent on strengthening freeways, bridges, and buildings in San Francisco to meet modern earthquake standards, today scores of the city's structures still await seismic reinforcement. Of particular concern are the numerous older apartment and office buildings that rest on un-reinforced garages, making them particularly susceptible to collapse during a major earthquake.

In 1906, about 650,000 people lived in the greater Bay Area, including the cities of Oakland and San Jose, with a little over 400,000 residing in San Francisco itself. Currently, the Bay Area has some 7 million inhabitants, more than 10 times as many as at the beginning of the twentieth century. Researchers estimate that if a 7.7–7.9 magnitude temblor involving the San Andreas Fault were to strike the San Francisco Bay Area today, nearly 100,000 structures would be damaged at a cost of $150 billion, up to 250,000 households would be displaced, some 12,000 individuals would be seriously injured, and between 2,000 and 3,500 would die.

Yet, although they are well aware that another "Big One" will assuredly strike the Bay Area again, wrote author Dan Kurzman, "as in 1906, few San Franciscans would live elsewhere." They choose to reside atop a seismic time bomb not because they are in a state of denial, but because they are convinced that the risks of living in one of the world's most beautiful and vibrant cities are worth the rewards. At the beginning of the twenty-first century, San Franciscans are prepared to face whatever challenges the future may bring them and their city with courage, hope, and perseverance, just as their ancestors did in 1906.

Chronology

1906   **Wednesday, April 18**

5:12–5:13 a.m.: 7.7–7.9 magnitude earthquake rocks San Francisco area; San Francisco fire chief, Dennis Sullivan, fatally injured.

Early morning: Within minutes of earthquake, more than 50 fires erupt in the city; General Funston orders all available troops to report to Hall of Justice.

Midmorning: "Ham and Eggs Fire" breaks out in western part of the city; dynamiting to create fire-breaks begins.

Timeline

Wednesday, April 18, 1906
Early morning: Within minutes of earthquake, more than 50 fires erupt in the city; General Funston orders all available troops to report to Hall of Justice

1906

Wednesday, April 18, 1906
5:12–5:13 a.m.: 7.7–7.9 magnitude earthquake rocks San Francisco area; San Francisco fire chief, Dennis Sullivan, fatally injured

Thursday, April 19, 1906
Fight to keep the fire from spreading west of Van Ness Avenue begins

Afternoon: South of Market Street area devastated by fire; San Francisco landmarks, the Call Building and Palace Hotel, burn; battle to save the U.S. Mint.

Evening: Fires north and south of Market Street and Ham and Eggs Fire merge; fourth major fire erupts at or near Delmonico's restaurant.

Thursday, April 19: Fight to keep the fire from spreading west of Van Ness Avenue begins.

Friday, April 20: Dynamiting of eastern side of Van Ness—or a shift in the wind—stops fire's advance westward but sends flames eastward toward Russian Hill and North Beach; Mission Hill fires halted in western and southern sections

1908
Report of the State Earthquake Investigation Commission is published

1909

Saturday, April 21, 1906
Fires finally brought under control on the waterfront early in the morning

1909
Most of the quake- and fire-devastated parts of San Francisco have been rebuilt

of the district; Navy Lieutenant Frederick Freeman and his men fight to save the north waterfront.

Saturday, April 21: Fires finally brought under control on the waterfront early in the morning.

1908   Report of the State Earthquake Investigation Commission is published.

1909   Most of the quake- and fire-devastated parts of San Francisco have been rebuilt.

1915   San Francisco hosts the Panama-Pacific International Exposition.

1989   On October 17, the 6.9 magnitude Loma Prieta earthquake strikes Bay Area.

Glossary

aftershocks   Less serious shocks that follow the main shock of the earthquake.

asthenosphere   Fluidlike layer of the Earth located just beneath the lithosphere.

backfire   A fire deliberately started in the path of a bigger, oncoming fire in an effort to take away its fuel and thereby extinguish it.

cable car   A type of passenger vehicle that operates on rails and is propelled by a moving underground cable.

cistern   Large underground tanks for storing water.

conscript   Draft.

draconian   Harsh; severe.

elastic rebound theory   The theory that earthquakes are created by strains that slowly accumulate in rock masses along faults. When the stresses become more powerful than the strength of the rocks, the pent-up energy is suddenly released with a jolt as the Earth's outer shell snaps like a rubber band stretched beyond its normal breaking point.

epicenter   The epicenter of an earthquake is the point on the Earth's surface directly above the focus.

fault   Weak spots in the Earth's outer shell; faults lie on the boundaries between the large rigid plates that make up the lithosphere.

firebreaks   Wide, empty spaces deliberately created in a large fire's path, typically by the dynamiting of buildings.

focus   The point beneath the Earth's surface where an earthquake originates.

graft   The use of political power for personal gain.

intensity   The intensity of an earthquake is the observed impact of the shaking on an area's buildings, natural features, and human inhabitants.

liquefaction   The process by which powerful earthquake waves can quickly reduce the firmness and strength of water-logged and loosely packed ground, leaving the shaken soil with the consistency of jelly.

lithosphere   The outer shell of the Earth; it is composed of a number of rigid, continuously moving plates or slabs.

made land   The term used by San Franciscans to describe the marshlands, underground creeks, and sections of San Francisco Bay that had been filled in with soil, sand, rocks, rotting timber, and other debris to create new residential and commercial areas for the growing city.

magnitude   The amount of energy released into the ground at an earthquake's focus or origin.

martial law   The temporary rule of an area by military authorities during an emergency when the normal civil authorities are judged unable to function effectively.

modified Mercalli scale   A scale for measuring the intensity of an earthquake, it eventually replaced earlier, less detailed intensity scales including the Rossi-Forel scale.

moment magnitude scale   Introduced in 1979, it has largely replaced the Richter scale for measuring the magnitude of an earthquake.

plate tectonics theory   A theory that states that Earth's lithosphere is made up of rigid, slowly moving plates and that earthquakes typically occur along faults on the borders of these plates.

Richter scale   A scale invented by seismologist Charles Richter in 1935 to rate the magnitude of earthquakes.

Rossi-Forel scale   A popular scale for measuring the intensity of an earthquake during the late nineteenth and early twentieth centuries.

San Andreas Fault   A long fault that runs along most of the western coast of California; plate movement along the fault was responsible for the San Francisco earthquake of 1906.

seismic waves   The vibrations sent out into the ground by an earthquake.

seismograph   A device that can detect and simultaneously record seismic waves from earthquakes.

seismology   A branch of science that studies all aspects of earthquakes.

temblor   An earthquake.

Bibliography

"...And Then The Fire Was Worse Than The Earthquake." *American History* 41 (April 2006): 34–35.

Bronson, William. *The Earth Shook, The Sky Burned.* Garden City, N.Y.: Doubleday, 1959.

Castleman, Michael. "Grace Under Fire." *Smithsonian*, April 2006, pp. 56–64.

Dvorak, John. "San Francisco Then and Now." *American Heritage*, April/May 2006, pp. 54–59.

Ewers, Justin. "Nightmare in San Francisco." *US News and World Report*, April 17, 2006, pp. 42–56

Fradkin, Philip L. *The Great Earthquake and Firestorms of 1906: How San Francisco Nearly Destroyed Itself.* Berkeley: University of California Press, 2005.

Hansen, Gladys, and Emmet Condon. *Denial of Disaster.* San Francisco: Cameron, 1989.

Hua, Vanessa. "Out of Chaos Came a New Chinese America." *San Francisco Chronicle*, April 13, 2006, p. A-1.

Iacopi, Robert L. *Earthquake Country: How, Why & Where Earthquakes Strike in California.* Tucson, Ariz.: Fisher Books, 1996.

Kurzman, Dan. *Disaster! The Great San Francisco Earthquake and Fire of 1906.* New York: HarperCollins, 2001.

Morris, Charles, ed. *The San Francisco Calamity by Earthquake and Fire.* Philadelphia: J.C. Winston, 1906.

Niderost, Eric. "California Catastrophe: The Great San Francisco Earthquake and Fire." *American History*, April 2006, pp. 28–38.

Nolte, Carl. "The Dynamite Disaster." *San Francisco Chronicle*, April 13, 2006, p. A-13.

———. "From Smoke and Ruin, a New City," *San Francisco Chronicle*, April 18, 2006, p. A-2.

———. "A Great City Reduced to Rubble," *San Francisco Chronicle*, April 16, 2006, p. A-12.

———. "The Great Fire." *San Francisco Chronicle*, April 12, 2006, p. A-11.

———. "The Quake Damage." *San Francisco Chronicle*, April 11, 2006, p. A-9.

———. "The Refugees." *San Francisco Chronicle*, April 14, 2006, p. A-21.

———. "Rising from the Ashes," *San Francisco Chronicle*, April 18, 2006, p. A-14.

———. "The Survivors." *San Francisco Chronicle*, April 17, 2006, p. A-8.

Pain, Elizabeth. "The Return of the 1906 Quake." *Science Now*, October 11, 2005, p. 3.

Perlman, David. "The Great Quake: 1906–2006: Quake Propelled Seismology." *San Francisco Chronicle*, April 11, 2006, p. A-1.

Rogers, Paul. "Ripples from 1906 San Francisco Quake Felt Even Today." *Seattle Times*, April 15, 2006.

Smith, Dennis. *San Francisco Is Burning: The Untold Story of the 1906 Earthquake and Fires*. New York: Viking, 2005.

Thomas, Gordon, and Max Morgan Witts. *The San Francisco Earthquake*. New York: Stein and Day, 1971.

Twain, Mark. *Roughing It*. Cutchogue, N.Y.: Buccaneer Books, 1976.

Winchester, Simon. *A Crack in the Edge of the World: America and the Great California Earthquake of 1906*. New York: HarperCollins, 2005.

WEB SITES

The Bancroft Library:

The 1906 San Francisco Earthquake and Fire

http://bancroft.berkeley.edu/collections/earthquakeandfire/search.html

Exploratorium: Great Shakes—San Francisco, 1906
http://www.exploratorium.edu/faultline/great/1906/index.html

Museum of the City of San Francisco:
    The Great Fire and Earthquake
http://www.sfmuseum.org/1906/06.html

National Geographic Eye in the Sky:
    Nature's Fury—Earthquakes
http://www.nationalgeographic.com/eye/earthquakes/
    earthquakes.html

National Park Service, Presidio of San Francisco:
    The 1906 Earthquake and Fire
http://www.nps.gov/archive/prsf/history/1906eq/index.htm

San Francisco Department of Public Health:
    The 1906 Earthquake and Fire, Bubonic Plague
http://www.dph.sf.ca.us/1906/plague/default.htm

The Tech Museum of Innovation: Earthquakes
http://www.thetech.org/exhibits_events/online/quakes/intro/

U.S. Geological Survey:
    The Great San Francisco Earthquake
http://earthquake.usgs.gov/regional/nca/1906/18april/index.php

Wells Fargo:
    Guided by History, Interactive Tour, San Francisco 1906
http://blog.wellsfargo.com/guidedbyhistory/Tour/index.html

Further Reading

Bronson, William. *The Earth Shook, The Sky Burned*. Garden City, N.Y.: Doubleday, 1959.

Chippendale, Lisa A. *The San Francisco Earthquake of 1906*. Philadelphia: Chelsea House, 2001.

Erickson, Jon. *Quakes, Eruptions, and Other Geologic Cataclysms*. New York: Facts On File, 2001.

Kusky, Timothy. *Earthquakes*. New York: Facts on File, 2008.

Levine, Ellen. *If You Lived at the Time of the Great San Francisco Earthquake*. New York: Scholastic, 1992.

Tanaka, Shelley. *Earthquake! April 18, 1906*. New York: Hyperion Books, 2004.

Van Meter, Larry A. *Yerba Buena*. New York: Chelsea House, 2007.

Worth, Richard. *The San Francisco Earthquake*. New York: Facts On File, 2005.

Picture Credits

Index

A

Active (tugboat), 74, 76
aftershocks, 79, 82
Agnews State Hospital, 38
alarms, 55, 105
Alaska, 53
American Red Cross, 83–85
American Society of Civil
   Engineers, 96
Army. *See* U.S. Army
Austin, Mary, 89

B

backfires, 68–69
Balboa, Vasco Núñez de, 102
Bank of America, 98
Bank of Italy, 97–98
banks, 97–98
Barbary Coast, 19–20
Barrett, John, 32–33
Bay Bridge, 107–108
Bernhardt, Sarah, 18
birth certificates, 77–78, 93–94
Booth, Edwin, 18
bribery, 21
Brownie cameras, 9
bubonic plague, 104–105
building codes, 104, 106
buildings, survival of, 35–38
Burnham, Daniel H., 92
Bush Street fire station, 54–55

C

cable cars, 22–23, 91
Call Building, 62–63
cameras, 9
Caruso, Enrico, 18
Chabot Observatory, 42

China, 43
Chinatown, 19–20, 91, 93–95,
   104–105
Chinese Exclusion Act, 19–20
cisterns, 25, 107
citizenship, 93–94
City Hall, 36–38, 58, 77, 102–103
Civic Center, 102
Cohen, Moshe, 65, 88
Columbus, Christopher, 13
Committee of Fifty, 59, 66, 83
Committee of Forty, 83, 85
Comstock Lode, 16–17
conscription, 86
construction methods, survival
   and, 35–38
Cook, Jesse, 7, 29–30
corruption, 20–26, 36–38, 103
cottages, earthquake, 96–97, 99
Custom House, 74
Cypress Street Viaduct, 108

D

Davis Street, 29–30
death tolls, 10, 43, 50, 77–78, 108
Devine, Edward, 85
Dewey, Guion, 94–95
Dinan, Jeremiah, 58
disaster preparation, 103–107
Doughtery, John, 61, 66
duration of earthquake, 10
duration of fire, 10
dynamite, use of, 9, 59–61, 67–70

E

earthquake cottages, 96–97, 99
East Street, 74
Eastman Kodak Company, 9

elastic rebound theory, 44–46
epicenter of earthquake, 47–48
evacuations, 71, 78–81
explosives, use of, 9, 59–61, 67–70
extortion, 21, 103

F
fatalities, 10, 43, 50, 77–78, 108
faults, 8, 42–46, 110
ferries, 79–80
Ferry Building, 79
filled land, 32–35, 47, 104, 108
fire fighters, 23–25
fire hydrants
    Dennis Sullivan and, 24–25
    lack of water to, 9, 55, 67
    redesign of after disaster,
        105–107
    working, 71
fireboats, 107
firebreaks, attempts to create, 9,
    59–61, 67–70
fire-limits building zone,
    104–105
firestorms, 62–63
Forel, François, 49
Fort Mason, 58, 85
Fradkin, Phillip, 96
Freeman, Frederick, 72–76
Funston, Frederick, 57–58, 59,
    64, 69

G
gas mains, 108
Giannini, Amadeo, 97–98
Gold Rush, 14–15, 103
Golden Gate Park, 18, 28, 82,
    84–85, 92
graft, 20–26, 36–38, 103
Grand Opera House, 18
Graves, H.C., 91

H
Hall of Justice, 102
Ham and Eggs Fire, 57, 65
Hanks, Tom, 51
Hansen, Gladys, 78
Harte, Bret, 18
Hayes Valley, 57
Hom, Marlon, 95
Hooker, Marion Osgood, 89
Hopper, James, 63
Horsburgh, James, 100
Hunt, Ralph, 56–57
Hunters Point, 93
hydrants
    Dennis Sullivan and, 24–25
    lack of water to, 9, 55, 67
    redesign of after disaster,
        105–107
    working, 71

I
insurance payouts, 98
intensity, determination of, 48–51

J
Japan, 41
Jorgensen, John, 88
Judson, Clarence, 28–29

K
Kanamori, Hiroo, 51–53
Keohane, Nellie, 62–63

L
Labor Union Party, 21
land fills, 32–35, 47, 104, 108
Langdon, William, 26
Latin Quarter, 19, 70, 71–72
Lawson, Andrew C., 42, 44
Lawson Report, 46–47
Leale, Marion, 79–81

Leslie (fireboat), 74, 76
liquefaction, 33–34
lithosphere, 45–46
loans, 98
Loma Prieta earthquake, 107–109
London, Jack, 9, 18, 65, 68–69,
    79–81
looters, shooting of, 58, 60, 86–87

M

made land, 32–35, 47, 104, 108
magnitude, 41, 48, 51–53, 108
Mare Island, 74
Marina District, 108
Market Street, 31, 36, 56–57, 70
martial law, 86–88
Mason, Fort, 58, 85
Mechanics' Pavilion, 82–83
Memorial Arch, 39
Mercalli, Guiseppe, 49
metal-framed buildings, 35–36
Mexico, 14
military, 86–88. *See also* U.S. Army
mint, 64–65, 97
Mission Delores, 71
Mission District, 71, 90
Modified Mercalli (MM)
    Intensity Scale, 49–51
Moment Magnitude Scale, 51–53
Montgomery Block, 74

N

National City (steamship), 28
Nob Hill, 18
North American plate, 46
North Beach District, 19, 70, 71–72
North of Market Fire, 65

O

Oakland, 79, 93, 96, 107
Older, Fremont, 25–26, 103

Olema, 47
opera, 18
opium dens, 20
Oriental City, 93

P

Pacific plate, 46
Palace Hotel, 31, 35–36, 63–64,
    94–95
Palo Alto, 38, 39
Panama Canal, 102
Panama-Pacific International
    Exposition, 102, 108
Pardee, George, 42, 46, 86, 88, 100
Parquette, Edmond, 37
parrots, 80–81
Phelan, James D., 59, 85, 103
phoenix, 103
phosphorescence, 29
photographic coverage, 9
plague, 104–105
plate tectonics, 44–46
politics, 20–26
Polk, Willis, 96
Pond, John, 72–73
Portolá, Gaspar de, 13–14
Portsmouth Square, 74
Preble, U.S.S., 74
preparation for future disasters,
    103–107
Presidio, 14, 58, 61, 82–83, 85,
    93, 99
Prince William Sound, 53
property damage estimates, 10
public relations campaign, 99–100
pumping stations, auxiliary, 107

R

railroads, 17, 18, 74, 79–80, 91–92,
    100
Ralston, William, 36, 63–64

Raymond, G.A., 31–32
rebuilding, 92, 95–99, 102, 104
Red Cross, 83–85
refugee camps, 85–86
Reid, Henry Fielding, 44, 46
reservoirs, storage, 107
Richter, Charles, 51–53
Richter Scale, 51–53
Rockefeller, John D., 84
Rolph, James, 103
Roosevelt, Theodore, 25, 83–85,
  86, 93
Rossi, Michele de, 49
Rossi-Forel intensity scale, 49
row houses, 105
rubble, clearing of, 90–93
Ruef, Abraham, 21–23, 25–26, 59,
  103
Russian Hill District, 70, 71–73,
  75

S

safety, reconstruction and, 104,
  110
sailors, 27–28
St. Francis Hotel, 95
St. Ignatius church, 78
San Andreas Fault, 8, 42–46, 110
San Francisco
  Chinatown, Barbary Coast
    and, 18–20
  Dennis Sullivan and, 23–25
  financial and cultural
    importance of, 15–18
  Fremont Older and, 25–26
  politics in, 20–23
  rise of, 13–15
San Francisco Bulletin, 25
San Francisco-Oakland Bay
  Bridge, 107–108
San Jose, 38

San Mateo, 98
sanitation, 85–86
Santa Cruz, 107
Santa Rosa, 38, 47, 49
Schmitz, Eugene
  corruption of, 21–23, 103
  crusade to topple, 25–26
  demolition and, 69–70
  "shoot-to-kill" order of,
    58–59, 60
  U.S. Army, Red Cross and,
    83–84
  Van Ness Avenue and, 66
Secret Service, 25
Sedgwick, Charles, 90
seismographs, 41–42, 47, 51
seismology
  elastic rebound theory and,
    44–46
  intensity of quake and, 48–51
  magnitude of quake and,
    51–53
  State Earthquake
    Investigation Commission
    and, 42–44, 46–48
  state of at time of quake,
    40–42
Shaughnessy, Patrick, 66
"shoot-to-kill" order, 58, 60,
  86–87
silver rush, 16–17
soil liquefaction, 33–34
South of Market Fire, 61
South of the Slot district, 18–20,
  33–34, 47, 55, 62
Southern Pacific Company, 100
Southern Pacific Railroad, 74, 79,
  91–92
Spain, 13–14
spontaneous combustion, 97
Spreckels, Rudolph, 25, 59, 103

Stanford University, 38, 39, 42
State Earthquake Investigation
    Commission, 42–44, 46–48, 100
statistics
    deadliest earthquakes since
        1900 (world) and, 43
    deadliest earthquakes (U.S.)
        and, 50
    earthquake and fire and, 10
    fire damage and, 76
    future earthquake estimates
        and, 110
    highest-magnitude
        earthquakes (U.S.) and, 48
    highest-magnitude
        earthquakes (world) and,
        41
Stevenson, Robert Louis, 18
Sullivan, Dennis, 23–25, 54, 61
Sullivan, Margaret, 54
Sutter's Mill, 14–15
swimmer, 27–29

T
tectonic plates, 44–46
Tiburon, 71
time of earthquake, 10
tourism, 94–95
Townsend Street, 74
transcontinental railroad, 17
tugboats, 74, 76

Twain, Mark, 16–17, 18
Twin Peaks, 107

U
United Railroads, 91–92
United States Mint, 64–65, 97
University of California at
    Berkeley, 42
U.S. Army
    calling for assistance of,
        57–58
    demolition and, 70
    martial law and, 86–88
    refugee camps and, 85–86
    relief camps and, 83
    "shoot-to-kill" order and, 58,
        60, 88–89

V
Valencia Street Hotel, 34–35
Van Ness Avenue, 18, 66–71
Viavi Company Complex, 70

W
Washington Street, 29
water. *See* Hydrants
Wellington (Steamship), 28
Western Addition, 66, 70, 90

Y
Yerba Buena settlement, 14

About the Author

LOUISE CHIPLEY SLAVICEK received her master's degree in history from the University of Connecticut. She is the author of numerous periodical articles and 20 books for young people, including *Women of the American Revolution*, *Israel*, and *Carlos Santana*. She lives in Ohio with her husband, James, a research biologist, and their two children, Krista and Nathan.

WITHDRAWN